CW00762953

A PRACTICAL GUIDE FROM THE 5-STAR HOSPITALITY SECTOR

5-STAR

EXPERIENCE MARKETING

FOR DENTISTS

BY SHAZ MEMON

5-STAR

EXPERIENCE MARKETING

FOR DENTISTS

BY SHAZ MEMON

This book was published in 2023 by Verb Press.

Connect with Shaz Memon:

Website shaz.co.uk
Instagram instagram.com/shaz.memon instagram.com/digimax.dental instagram.com/clin.ics
LinkedIn linkedin.com/in/shazmemon

CONTENTS

Scan to stay updated

A U T H O R

SHAZ / MEMON

Founder of Digimax Dental

Founder of Wells on Wheels

Founder of Clinics.co.uk

Shaz Memon is the founder of Digimax Dental in London. The world's highest-rated dental marketing agency. An astute business leader, designer, and award-winning dental marketing expert. Shaz was voted 15th most influential person in UK Dentistry and has been featured in leading publications, including Forbes, Channel 5 News, BBC, Daily Mail, Reuters, The Independent, Newsweek, Times of India, TRT World, Daily Express, and The Guardian. Shaz also founded the charity Wells on Wheels, providing water wheels to villages in India.

shaz.memon
London, United Kingdom

wells on wheels
wells.on.wheels
Maharashtra, India

Wells on Wheels

Founded by Shaz Memon, Wells on Wheels helps families in rural regions of India. Women of all ages, including young girls, walk an average of 1-2 miles a day, carrying water on their heads from the source back to their communities. Over time, the weight leads to chronic neck and back pain, with musculoskeletal disorders sometimes leading to complications during childbirth. Women may be pregnant or carrying a baby on their back in addition to their load. Young girls miss out on their childhood and don't get to attend school.

The water wheel is a large, round drum that is fitted with handles so it can be rolled along the ground with ease. These containers enable water collectors to roll liquid from wells rather than carry it on their heads. It can hold up to five times more water than a single bucket, reducing the number of trips needed and eliminating the burden on the head, back, and neck.

10% of proceeds from the sale of this book will go towards helping these women and girls (sometimes as young as seven years old), who must walk miles in the blazing heat to transport water to survive.

Let's ease the burden on our mothers, sisters, and daughters.

One wheel costs £28 including logistics. I hope this book helps you as much as your purchase helps us to provide Wells on Wheels to those who need it most.

Learn more by following **@wells.on.wheels** and visiting **wellsonwheels.co.uk**

Introduction

It can take decades to build a great reputation, but it takes just moments to ruin it. Thousands of £££ spent on marketing is not going to magically grow your practice or increase the FREE referrals your practice could receive.

There is a minority of dental clinics...

- Whose dental work is high-quality
- Whose customer acquisition is effortless
- Whose operating standards are impeccable

And their patients?

- Admire them
- Love them
- Rave about them (beyond just Google reviews!)...

...but in private as well:

They tell their friends and family about their experience – no, they 'insist' that their friends see YOU to experience your incredible service, care, and treatment. The difference here is that this will go up significantly in volume if you nail your customer service experience at the practice.

This minority of practices have a few fundamental things in common that mediocre dental practices overlook, and therefore, struggle with consistent, predictable, and profitable brand growth...

That fundamental thing is delivering '5-star customer service' to every patient.

5-star customer service is about attitude, attention, systems and consistency. This level of customer service isn't necessarily associated with practices that are marble-clad, dripping in gold trimmings, and in parts of town where people may also enjoy a Salt Bae steak. This level of customer service is seen even in the smallest of private practices as well as private focused mixed practices, in unassuming towns across the UK.

The strategies in this book will teach you to

- Grow your dental brand without spending a penny more on marketing
- Turn your practice into the most raved-about dental practice in your town and city
- Leave your competitors so far behind that they have no idea how to catch up
- Stop relying solely on expensive cold leads

There is a pre-requisite. An obvious one that I must state. Your product must be outstanding, in dental terms, your dentistry must be of a high quality. I am sure it is, else you wouldn't have purchased this book.

The guidance in this book draws inspiration from 5-star hotels worldwide, all of which are covered in our course on **clinics.co.uk**.

Customer service isn't something you do, it's something you become. Let's begin.

Why did I write this book?

I wanted to write this book to emphasise that I truly believe there is no better marketing return on investment than investing time in building up your customer service standards to a 'wow' standard.

It has taken more than 20 years to learn some things that seem glaringly obvious to me now, that don't seem to be obvious to the majority of businesses around us, especially in today's broken world.

I am the founder of Digimax Dental. The world's highest-rated dental marketing agency. We design the world's most powerful dental websites (websites that make our clients more profit using a proven formula) and are also beautiful, which is a by-product. Powerful first-page Google rankings (SEO) and practice branding.

There is no point in prioritising investment in websites, SEO, and clever marketing campaigns if your customer service levels are not quite up to par. There, I've said it, even at the risk of losing business.

I implemented everything I have learned to change the trajectory for my business, Digimax, and every business I am a part of. As a marketer, I can see that customer service is the only sure-fire way to accelerate and future-proof any business and I want you to do the same for your dental practice.

A few years from starting out, I had built up momentum. I was still early in my journey. With a few dental clients under my belt, I knew what I was doing and had a passion I couldn't see in my competitors. Then, a potential client approached me and shared her idea: to create one of the most beautiful practices ever seen.

Every sentence she spoke sparked an explosion of ideas in my mind. She had to give me this project and I was prepared to work long and hard to win it.
She told me: 'Shaz, I don't think anyone but you can fulfil my vision.'

I simply said: 'I won't let you down.'

This was going to turn out to be the first lie I told her.

I got to work almost immediately. Ideas always come to my mind, and I don't need weeks to think about how to execute them – this is still true today. There was an animation style I had in mind. I didn't know how to execute it, but I knew how I wanted it to look.

So, I set about designing the best possible piece of work I'd ever created. Every ounce of design energy, passion, love, and knowledge that I had to give went into this project. This is no exaggeration. I moved things, changed things, moved them back. It went on for a long time until I reached perfection.

Some say, there is no such thing as perfection. And I can agree in the right context... but this was different. And, as you get to the end, you will understand why I can say this.

Having doubts

Sunrise a few hours after I had finished, I had set my alarm to email the client. I didn't want to send an email at 4am – I felt it would appear unprofessional.

So, I waited until 8am to press send.

And then I waited. A whole day had passed...and I was thinking my work hadn't pleased her.

Why wouldn't she like it? Maybe I am not cut out for this.

But I am. I know it was amazing.

Why hadn't she come back to me yet if she loved it? I give up...

All these conversations were happening in my mind until she called me the next morning after a very uncomfortable night's sleep.

Client: 'Shaz, I didn't want to email you. Emailing wouldn't be fair on you.'

My mind: 'Oh God....don't...'

Client: 'I couldn't have even in my dreams imagined a design like this was even possible. My mind is blown. I can't even find the words.'

She went on to ask me how I did certain parts, and what inspired me.

I felt we were alike – hugely passionate about her business and brand, and she said: 'My patients are going to absolutely love this. Thank you so much, Shaz!'

I slept comfortably that evening and continued to complete the project. This was back in 2009 and it is a website I am still proud of today.

Fast forward five months, the client reached out to me for a website update. She had to add a new team member to the website.

I replied instantly: 'No problem, I will get this done for you.'

I was working alone, and when you are good at what you do, it really doesn't take long for people to start recommending Digimax (just me at the time). Like this project, many others were coming in all with their own dreams and aspirations and all with their own pressures.

And then I get a follow-up email. It read: 'Shaz, any news on my update?'

I didn't respond right away because I believed it would be better to email her right after I had made the update she had requested.

Another day passed and I still hadn't completed the update as I was busy on other projects. I knew making the website update was important. But I was prioritising new projects.

One of the biggest mistakes I would ever make!

Two days passed and, in my mind, I 100% knew I would make the website update. But I just didn't take it seriously as I thought it's not a big deal if it takes me a few days to add a team member to the site.

I thought to myself that the hard work was done, the site is amazing, it's online and it's working – I will get around to it.

The client emailed me: 'Shaz, thank you so much for the website. You did a great job. I have been speaking to a friend and she has given me the contact of a larger company that will be taking over the website and will be able to offer me a prompter service. Thank you again for everything.'

I had just created the best website possible. She even said herself she had never seen anything like it – yet she was going to leave for another company over a minor website update.

There was no changing her mind. She had decided.

And, after the polite email and many exchanges, she frankly felt let down. I still felt it was a major overreaction. I felt she was ungrateful for my efforts and that it was wrong of her to want to leave.

It took me weeks of thinking about this situation with no real closure. To add salt to the wound, the new company that took over had removed 'Designed by Digimax' from the footer of the website and changed it to their company name.

Whilst mourning the loss and nursing the anger about someone else passing off my work as their own, I happened to stumble upon this line: 'The little things, are the big things.'

I realised one of the most important lessons in business I may ever learn.

A client's expectations of you are just as important once the project is complete (aftercare) as they are at the beginning and throughout the process. A completely transferrable concept to dentistry.

I let the client down because I was naive enough to think her update was not that important. But, in truth, it wasn't my decision to make.

I lost a client over it, and future business to a competitor.

I told myself at that point: I will never let this happen again. The customer service in my company will be world-class.

As I built Digimax, every team member heard this customer service lesson on every onboarding. Any opportunity I received to use this story, I did.

However, deep down, I still didn't have closure. But since then, I have never had a client leave for this reason.

I have established an exceptional customer service team within my aftercare department that prioritises prompt website updates, unlike the situation mentioned above. This team is dedicated to swiftly delivering updates and is equipped with ample resources. Digimax clients consistently praise the unparalleled level of aftercare they receive, surpassing their past experiences with other web companies.

Fast forward 10 years, and an email arrives at Digimax.

Introducing the new Digimax – a company that has evolved, grown stronger, and expanded significantly, now equipped with advanced customer service systems. We have come a long way from embryonic beginnings in a garage.

The same passion that gave me growth is what I injected into building every moving part of the business we have today. All our customer service systems, ways of thinking, values, and culture are the result of harsh lessons like the one I experienced above.

The email enquiry is from the same practice I lost 10 years ago because my communication was not good enough.

My eyes widened. I told my colleague: 'Do you remember that story about…' He finished my sentence: 'About how you lost a client because of the website update?'

I said: 'Yes, that one! How did you remember…'

He rolled his eyes 

'Well, they have enquired, and we will get this client, no matter what it takes. Please tell them that I remember them, and I want them back.'

I invited them to meet me in London. We spoke about what had happened.

I sheepishly said: 'I have been waiting for you for 10 years.'

They said: 'It's about time we had our website redesigned and the service we have been receiving with our current company has been shocking.'

They were leaving the company they were with for the same reason they left me…only to come back to me.

I asked: 'Would you like to see the website I made you 10 years ago?'

They were surprised I still had it. I showed them. They looked at each other and their eyes lit up.

Then, they asked me to place it side by side with their current website (only two years old) and they said (to which I agreed) that their old site is far more beautiful and powerful than their current website.

They even made a comment: 'Could we not just go back to this site?'
But I knew way too much about user behaviour and had learned a whole heap more in 10 years to accept that.

I told them about the lesson I had learned. I explained that thanks to them, I now have a culture that is hard to find elsewhere.

- Express website update service (subject to task complexity).
- A concierge service for clients after launch (no monthly fees for life).

- Five people in the website update team (when we could run with three).
- A quality control department to ensure website updates are done correctly.
- Training videos to self-update a website for immediate review if it's a weekend or late night and they need something done.

And most importantly, the team have been trained to communicate better than I did all those years back!

They were impressed.

I worked on their project and ensured they received the new Digimax service. Their project was a winner.

I asked them if they wanted to enter the Dental Website Awards, and they did. I received a picture from the awards night as I was unable to attend and they had won 'Best website, London' – one of the most competitive website categories to win in.

I learned from this, that a great website is expected. How we treat clients is where we make a difference and boost our reputation or damage our reputation. This is completely transferrable to your dental practice.

Through this story, I want you to see why I'm writing this book. The small actions in customer service are actually big moves that get noticed and lift your business. By taking thoughtful steps, establishing consistent systems, showing generosity and empathy, and excelling in communication, we create businesses that people talk about and succeed.

Formal customer service training

As a business leader, you learn many things that you go on to teach your team. Some of these lessons and approaches sound like they are landing, but often don't really register with your team. They are hearing you all the time, similar to when you are in your teens and your parents are forever guiding... You tend to just nod and say yes.

In praise of my team, they had become great. They really cared about every touchpoint with clients as they could see the evolution of the company, and how working at Digimax had changed from firefighting to just pure love and appreciation from clients. It was bizarre, but they trusted me to lead them to take Digimax into a new era.

By now, I was convinced that if I could excel in my craft of designing websites that genuinely increase profits for practices and prevent them from losing hundreds of thousands of pounds each year (which they aren't even aware of), then the only other way I could set Digimax apart is by establishing a standard of customer service that is unparalleled. Your patients naturally anticipate exceptional dentistry, as they may not fully comprehend the intricacies involved. It is how you deliver the overall experience that truly sets you apart and resonates with them.

When leaders visit other businesses, they do something quite different to most customers. When I visit a business of any kind, I am always assessing my experience, and wondering how some things work, how that team member is smiling, and another isn't. What systems do they have in place to make this lobby look gleaming 24/7? That door-man who greeted me like I am the only guest he has seen today – how is he keeping that up working over 40 hours a week in the cold?

ANNA
TOSCANA
Learn insider customer
service skills from the
hospitality industry
clinics

That's when it hit me... what if I get my team trained by trainers in the 5-star hospitality industry? Surely the concepts of making people feel consistently amazing are transferrable? While I wasn't 100% sure about this, I did want to explore it. With a bit of work, I managed to find one of Europe's leading hospitality industry training companies and asked for their best trainer. The trainer was an ex-concierge in some of the world's leading hotels – the level where he was assigned to work closely with dignitaries, royalty, and celebrities at any cost when they arrived at a property. I got to speak with him to see if he would consider training my team, and he responded with 'Absolutely, I would love to take on the challenge. It's different to what I would usually do but I have been saying all along 'Customer service from the 5-star hospitality industry, can easily be installed into any business'.

The trainer's name is Ramin. I took my team to his training course, and they were blown away by the level of thought that goes into the top hotels in the world. He didn't once tell us what to do, but he taught us how we should be thinking about customer service.

He said, 'Every interaction is an opportunity to wow'. Every story he shared from his concierge days, landed in a way where we could apply it to the way we treat our clients. We were mindblown and oozing with ideas. We made it a weekly task to come together and build our customer service systems.

His workbook allowed us to create our very own Customer Service Manual which later went on to be part of our award entry submissions, where we would go on to win numerous customer service awards inside and outside of the dental industry.

Ramin and I kept in touch. When our customer service systems matured, and I started to notice practices could really couple their powerful marketing with his customer service teachings, I knew I had to approach him with an offer. I asked Ramin to train other dental practices in the industry to improve patient experiences.

Initially, Ramin politely declined my offer. He was in high demand and enjoyed training hotel teams. However, when the pandemic hit and the hospitality industry came to a grinding halt, Ramin found himself with an uncertain future for the first time in 20 years. He knew the dental industry was in need of the same level of customer service excellence that he had been able to bring to the hospitality industry and decided to join me in training dental practices.

Through training, Ramin saw first-hand the lack of customer service team training and buy-in that led to poor patient experiences in many dental clinics. After Ramin trained my team, I asked him:

'A few things you delivered to the team today are something I have mentioned to them before. But they didn't register the information from me like they did with you. They acted like they heard it for the first time when you said it… and were super impressed.'

Ramin explained to me that this was the beauty of bringing in an expert with real credentials.

They bring a fresh perspective and new techniques that in-house training may not provide. This was especially true in the dental industry, where Ramin also found patient experiences to be weak overall.

With his experience training nearly a thousand 5-star luxury hotels, Ramin began to focus on training dental clinics on how to achieve the highest customer satisfaction possible. His methods have had an incredible impact on the reputation of these clinics, as patients value unexpected exceptional customer service above all else.

This is when we decided to come together and bring in-house training to dental practices. Visit **clinics.co.uk** to learn more.

This book teaches you and your team how you can learn from the hospitality industry, to grow your practice predictably using the resources you already may have.

Do you think patients come to you because you are a great dentist?

Most patients already think you are a great dentist.

They are already expecting high-quality dentistry, what they don't know is how you will wow them with a feeling of care, comfort, and detail – not just in the chair. From the first moment they enquire to the moment they enter your premises or begin a virtual consultation, to the second they step away and even to the next day and beyond, after their appointment.

Patients don't just recommend you because of the great dental care and results you achieve for them; you will find if you really dig deep that they liked coming to you and recommended you for a whole host of reasons. It could be something that happens as soon as they enter, a communication, a smell, a smile, or a personable conversation.

As time goes by, you will start to see a steady stream of new patients referred by your existing ones, without the need to actively request it! If you are already experiencing this, then the principles outlined in this book will have an even greater impact on you, considering you have already established a strong foundation.

In the United Kingdom, in particular, in most cases, you either get exactly what you are expecting from a business or less. You just need to walk into any restaurant, hotel lobby, or high street business to experience this. We are so used to atrociously basic customer service that the moment someone does anything more than the standard – we feel immense gratitude. Sometimes we are so taken aback that we will say thank you multiple times.

I am talking about lack of warmth, eye contact, and unclear answers, making us feel awkward, slam on the table service, making you wait, making you wonder, almost feeling stupid to ask kind of customer service, which is prevalent in the UK and most parts of the world.

'Ok fine! – I get it, I always have! But it's my team that doesn't understand!' Well don't blame them (yet), they don't know what they don't know. Let's start implementing the teachings in this book, turn these ideas into systems and then see if we can up their game. We will know soon enough if your team just don't want to improve, or if they simply needed direction and your leadership when it comes to making patients leave feeling wow.

Let me remind you, wow can come from the smallest of gestures. Disappointment can come from the lack of the smallest of gestures!

How can we make every patient feel like a celebrity?

I'm quite lucky with my clients. Yesterday, I worked with Lady Gaga in the morning, Raheem Sterling in the afternoon and Antonio Banderas in the evening. Hold on. Now I come to think of it; it wasn't actually them. It just felt like it was them. Allow me to explain.

When my partner and I stayed at a 5-star hotel in Chiang Mai, we were disappointed to discover that the sense of serenity in the 'serenity spa' was drowned out by noise from nearby construction. A small bit of feedback I gave to the team was that they should've alerted us ahead of our stay, so it didn't come as a surprise.

They responded by offering us complimentary dinner, and when we turned up at the hotel restaurant, we were greeted like celebrities. The best service we've ever received. We were welcomed with beaming smiles. All the waiters knew our names, and the chef came out to personally talk through the dishes and the menu. He even asked what we liked and brought us something perfectly tailored to our tastes.

We were so impressed; we decided to return the following day. The experience was completely different. The food was still delicious, and we were still treated well, but we weren't greeted by name.

No one smiled, and waiters walked past, only turning if we needed their attention. It's hard to explain, but the atmosphere was completely different. We were just regular folk having a good experience. There was no story to be told.

As we left the restaurant after that wonderful first night, it hadn't even occurred to me that the celebrity treatment was part of their attempt at service recovery. I thought the complimentary meal was the service recovery, and the treatment was simply how they treated everyone. I assumed this was the sort of place where everyone felt like a celebrity.

And this got me thinking. Why wasn't it the sort of place where everyone felt like a celebrity? And, more to the point, why aren't all customers made to feel this way when they go to a reputable establishment?

Making a conscious effort to ensure every client you work with is treated the same way you would treat Gaga, Sterling, Banderas, or any other celebrity name, is easily one of the best reputation-building exercises a business can make, with little or even no financial investment.

Creating wow moments can come from the smallest of actions. While running workshops, I noticed that most people have a difficult time arriving at a new venue. I thought to myself, what would I appreciate if I was in this situation? And so, at 6am on the event day, my team send a video by text message to each attendee showing them precisely what the walking route from the tube exit to the venue looks like. It's an eye-level view video of me doing the walk! Anticipating attendee's needs and taking the thinking out of the process means that they arrive relaxed and have an enjoyable experience.

In 5-star hotels, there's a feature in the guest management systems called profile notes. Profile notes are available to any team member and include preferences and other vital information that help deliver a 5-star experience. The concept of profile notes can be similarly utilised in a dental practice.

These could contain preferences about favourite drinks on arrival, choice of music during treatment, family member names, special upcoming events, or vacations the patients may have discussed. As a proactive team, you can act on this information.

As another example from my own experience, a client once called me to discuss a dental website design on behalf of her employer. Once we got talking, she shared with me that she was going to Los Angeles for the first time and was excited. So, I went on Amazon and sent her a city guide to Los Angeles. She was so wowed that she shouted about it on social media and even insisted her employer use us to design his website.

I've written previously about the curious phenomenon whereby businesses get repeat customers from people who initially complain about the service they have received. This is because the company goes to huge lengths to overcompensate for the error. It certainly makes sense to treat disappointed customers in this way, but why not make things easier for yourself by proactively extending this treatment to everyone? Celebrity endorsements can be a huge boost for any business. But if you create a culture where everybody is treated like a celebrity, you might find word spreads just as fast. Studies show that 51% of UK consumers trust recommendations from friends or partners more than any other brand advertising.

And, in today's world, with so many influential people around us, you never know when you might be serving someone who could have a huge impact on how your business is perceived. So come on, let's treat everyone like an A-lister. And who knows, maybe one day soon, you'll find yourself saying, 'I'm terribly sorry, Mr. Banderas, but we're booked up for months.'

To love their kids is to win their hearts

Following a series of flight alterations and delays, my family and I found ourselves unexpectedly stationed at a hotel in Frankfurt. It was merely a one-day layover, an unwanted pause in our journey to Japan, which still lay ahead in the distance. Our collective mindset was focused solely on weathering this transit period.

The hotel was the epitome of a generic, impersonal business hub, lacking warmth and character—just another waypoint for transient guests. The type of establishment that slips from your memory the moment you cross its threshold to depart. Since this was an unplanned part of our trip, we kept our expectations minimal. Although the hotel was well-situated and boasted a modern interior, it lacked a distinct element to make it memorable... until we encountered an exceptional gesture upon our arrival.

A delightful lady at the reception caught sight of my six-year-old daughter. Leaving her post, she approached us, kneeled to meet my daughter at eye level, and presented her with a card. It was a voucher for a complimentary mocktail of her choice from the hotel bar. My daughter's face was a picture of surprise and delight; she felt remarkable and special. She hurried us through the check-in process, eager to explore the bar and create her own drink. The sequence of receiving the card, anticipating the bar visit, choosing her colourful drink, and finally, sitting down to savour her creation, set a positive tone for our stay. This single, thoughtful act transformed a forgettable travel experience into a cherished memory for my daughter and us.

Will we remember this hotel? Unquestionably. Would we recommend it? Absolutely. Would our review be favourable? It would be more than that—it would be glowing. And all because they directed their attention to the most precious little person in our lives. The lesson is clear: show care and attention to people's children, and the parents may reciprocate with their attention—and their appreciation.

Emphasis on exceeding

One recurring theme you'll notice throughout this book is an emphasis on exceeding. I can't emphasise the importance of it enough!

You have heard of the concept 'under promise, over deliver' at some point in life. It is a business strategy of delivering your patients a service or experience above and beyond what you promised them. When you exceed their expectations by 'overdelivering', you make them feel valued and respected.

In everything you do, in everything your team does, you should always be asking yourself, 'How can we make this a better experience for our patients?'

Have you placed thought into every touch point a patient has? Has the standard of your treatment met or exceeded the results they were expecting to see? Did you explain exactly how they may feel after treatment and how they can contact you? Did you create a patient experience that would be uncommon to receive in the practice nearby?

Samuel Walton, the founder of the world's largest superstore chain, Walmart, once advised, 'Exceed your customer's expectations. If you do, they'll come back over and over. Give them what they want – and a little bit more'.

So, start asking yourself, 'How can I give that little bit more'?

Create wow moments!

As team members, you are constantly presented with opportunities to go above and beyond for your patients.

Creating and successfully delivering a wow moment isn't about the act itself but rather the impact that 'wow' moment has on your patient. Every patient will be different and react differently to different situations. For example, one person may perceive an offer of refreshments on arrival as standard but not particularly special or unexpected. At the same time, another patient might be entirely wowed by the friendly welcome, hospitality, and wide range of beverages.

Wow moments need to be consistent. If you only offer refreshments on a patient's first visit but not the second, they will feel like the 'service' has gone down. Similarly, the wow factor can wear off. A patient may be charmed by how well-designed and welcoming your practice is, but by their 3rd or 4th visit, that wow factor may be diminished, so you will need to delight them in different ways. Whilst it may be diminished for some, do realise that it will still be expected!

You and your team should always be alert to opportunities that allow you to provide wow moments. When you anticipate your patient's needs, when you are proactive and intentional about it, you turn it into a habit; and thinking creatively of ways to make people happy and improve their day is a great habit to have!

Grow your practice for free

One of the greatest things about exceptional customer service is that it needn't be expensive. Simply elevating the attention of care, communication, and small details costs almost nothing, but the impact it can have in terms of patient trust is limitless.

Outstanding customer service will lead to increased patient loyalty and retention. Once they've had an experience that stands out, they're more likely to talk about you to others and return. Statistics show that 89% of consumers are more likely to make another purchase after a positive customer service experience.

As a result, you can expect more positive word-of-mouth recommendations, social media endorsements, and glowing Google reviews that will further enhance your reputation and build trust around your brand. With so much choice, patients are consciously making choices to go with practices that have built up a strong reputation of going that extra bit further.

Phenomenal customer service will set you apart from your competitors. Patients aren't just buying into a specific treatment; they're buying an experience. Sometimes they don't know this until they begin the journey. With customer experiences in the UK being so lukewarm, when you make the effort to do that much more than what your competitors are willing to do – expect your patients to notice.

There is no question that prioritising customer service standards and systems in your practice will affect your bottom line. Word of mouth is already the biggest source of traffic for most practices, now imagine putting that on steroids. No amount of marketing spend can beat a practice that has an army of patients going out of their way to speak about you to others. Research has shown that 84% of organisations working to improve customer service reported an increase in revenue.

Customer service by numbers

89%
increase in purchases after a positive customer service experience
Salesforce Research

93%
of repeat purchases are increased by excellent customer service
HubSpot Research

78%
return after a mistake if company has excellent customer service
Salesforce Research

83%
of customers feel more loyal to brands that respond to complaints
Khoros

12
positive experiences are needed to counteract one negative experience
Ruby Newell-Legner

78%
of customers backed out after a poor experience
Glance

62%
recommend a brand if provided with exceptional service
Gladly

83%
of consumers cite good customer service as the most important factor
Khoros

58%
of consumers believe customer experience is a deciding factor
Sitel Group

50%
of consumers will switch to a competitor after one negative experience
Talkative

80%
will switch to a competitor after more than one negative experience
Zendesk

75%
of customers are willing to pay more for a good experience
Zendesk

21%
profitability increase in teams who are highly engaged
Gallup

75%
of customers expect personalisation
Yieldify

68%
of customers will spend more with brands that understand them
Khoros

KNOW YOURSELF, KNOW YOUR PATIENTS

GOOD
VIBES
ONLY
WHAT IS YOUR STORY?

Know your brand

Your brand is the very essence of your practice. It is your patient's perception of you, your treatments, and your quality. It is who you are. It is what tells potential patients why they should come to your practice, over your competitors.

Only when you have a deep understanding of your brand and what it is that sets you apart from your competitors can you deliver outstanding customer service to your patients. To gain this understanding, ask yourself:

1. What is the purpose of your practice? What motivates you to get out of bed every day? Many dental teams can describe what they do, but not always why they do it. So, ask yourself why you are in this business.
2. What is your brand story? This includes not only the history of your practice but also your values, mission, purpose, and successes.
3. Who are your patients, and what impression do they have of your brand?
4. What personality traits are you conveying to your current and potential patients?
5. What unique benefits do you offer to your patients? How are you different from your competitors? What makes you stand out in your market?

Transforming these questions into a team-building activity can create a sense of ownership and belonging among your practice staff. A robust brand will also inspire and guide your employees in providing outstanding customer service. If your team members don't understand your brand identity or values, it's difficult to expect patients to grasp them. Strong branding and company values play a crucial role in helping you connect with your patients emotionally and with clarity and focus.

Your brand is not the same as your brand identity, which encompasses visual elements like your logo, typography, brand colours, and website design (something my company Digimax Dental can help with). Instead, your brand is you. It embodies what you have to offer, your story, your vision, and your voice. Understanding your brand means knowing who you are, who you aspire to become, and how your patients perceive you.

Know your patients

Knowing and understanding who your patients are is crucial to understanding the type of experience they can expect and how you, as a dental professional, can best service their needs efficiently, effectively, and most importantly, with exceptional customer service.

Understanding your patients' perspective is crucial in creating a personalised and enjoyable patient experience. Knowing more than just their names – understanding their lives, hobbies, tastes, and interests – allows you to personalise every interaction. Asking patients about their loved ones, family, children, or pets, ensuring you have their favourite drink available, and playing their preferred music in the treatment room are examples of this personalisation. Building trust and loyalty through personalisation forms the foundation of a strong patient relationship.

The easiest way to get to know your patients is to listen! Any interaction you have, from small talk in the waiting room to consultations in the treatment rooms, is an opportunity to know your patients better. Snippets of information that your patients may view as idle chit-chat can inform you of their personal lives. They may talk about their friends and family or about things they do and don't like, and every piece of information you glean can be utilised to deliver incredible experiences.

You should be proactive in getting to know your patients. Ask them questions! Ask for feedback (**See page 293**) and engage with them on social media (with consent). While many people may enjoy talking about themselves, it is important to respect the privacy and comfort of each patient too. Gathering information about a patient's interests and preferences can be a great way to personalise the customer experience on their next visit. However, it is essential to use this information ethically and, with the patient's permission, and in compliance with data protection regulations. Knowledge is power; the more you know, the more powerful your customer service can become.

The patient perspective

The first touchpoint for any patient may be the marketing messages that your practice is broadcasting. This touchpoint can take many forms, from traditional offline marketing campaigns and word-of-mouth recommendations to your website, Google, and social media presence. Your patient's journey starts here. Your brand and identity, the language you use, and what you offer should align with your ideal patient's needs and desires from this point.

When a patient decides to enter your process, their mind will be full of questions, concerns, and perhaps even doubts. Answering these questions is an essential part of the process that you should be expecting and prepared for. However, every touchpoint in their journey, such as how you answer the phone, reply to emails, greet them in person, or describe your treatments, will also shape their experience. Exceptional customer service can alleviate any questions without the patient needing to vocalise their concerns. On the other hand, poor customer service can turn one concern into ten, leaving a long-lasting negative impression.

For instance, when responding to emails, make sure to use enthusiastic language and reply in a prompt manner, as even a brief, real acknowledgement email (not an auto-response) will have a positive impact. **See page 130 on 5-star email etiquette**.

Just like a production line, every aspect of the patient experience should appear effortless and flawless. A breakdown in any one part can have a negative impact on everything else. Any interruptions or delays, even during the initial consultation, can influence the decision-making and future recommendation process. Remember, every interaction with a patient counts as a touchpoint, and the chapters in this book are intended to guide you on how to make each one count!

The cost of brain calories in patient experience

Imagine walking through an airport where none of the boarding gates were clearly numbered. If so, you can imagine the frustration, nerves, and stress it can cause. Every time you must stop and think about something, you expend a 'brain calorie.'

The same principle applies to patient experience. The more brain calories a patient must burn to understand something about your practice, location, treatment, or processes, the more challenging the experience becomes. Patients don't want to burn energy deciphering complex systems or navigating confusing websites. They want to focus on their desired outcome and get the care they need.

To provide a seamless patient experience, it's crucial to think about the businesses that make your life easy. For example, Amazon's 'one-click' ordering system or Apple's intuitive user interface. These companies have streamlined their processes to make things effortless for their customers. Patients should receive the same level of ease and convenience when interacting with your practice.

Every 1% improvement in reducing the amount of thinking a patient needs to do can have a significant impact on their overall experience. So, it's essential to make it easy for patients to do business with you. Clear signage, simple directions, parking guidance, user-friendly websites, and intuitive booking processes all contribute to reducing cognitive load for patients, marking the beginning of a smooth, more satisfying experience.

Make it easy to do business with you.

High-value patient standards

As a society, we have never been more invested in our appearance and health. In 2021, the health & beauty market size in the UK was worth £36.7 billion, with cosmetic dentistry accounting for £2.2 billion of that. People want to look good and feel good, and they're willing to pay for the best treatments on offer.

Some high-value patients who come to your practice for treatments may expect a certain level of service. To make these patients feel extra valued and to encourage them to speak positively about your practice in their inner circles, it's crucial to provide exceptional customer service that exceeds their expectations. Striving to exceed the service they could receive as a VIP at a 5-star hotel is a great way to think about achieving this. While not all high-value patients may have indulgent tastes, no patient would complain about being treated exceptionally well.

Everything you offer at your practice for these patients should match the standard they will be accustomed to from other brands they respect and praise.

The basics:

- Greet them by name and with a smile the way concierges do at the top hotels
- Remember their favourite drinks the way that maître d's do at Michelin-star restaurants
- Be attentive and caring and make sure they have everything they need to be relaxed and comfortable the way business class air hostesses do

These patients need to move through their days seamlessly with no interruption to the level of service they are used to at every turn, so don't let your practice be the business they lower their standards for. Make sure that on their way to, during, and after every treatment, each element of their experience aligns with the high-value and exceptional standards that you have promised them.

To be talked about within your patients' inner circles, with some even insisting that friends and family travel outside of their area to see you, it's essential to pay attention to the little details that many other practices overlook.

Customer service impact on revenue

It's a fact that people will pay more for better service. According to research by PwC, 86% of buyers are willing to pay more for a great customer experience.

In the dental industry, where there is plenty of choice and competition, the price is seldom the only decisive factor that determines whether a patient selects your practice over a competitor's. Your customer service, the overall patient experience, and the way you make patients feel are all vital considerations. These elements are conveyed not only through your marketing but also through what others say about your practice, particularly those who have experienced your customer service standards.

While a first-class seat on an airplane may not get you to your destination any faster, it will undoubtedly provide a more comfortable journey, superior treatment, and better meals compared to economy class. Even on budget airlines, customers are willing to pay extra for priority boarding or more legroom. Similarly, those who opt for Amazon Prime are willing to pay more for faster deliveries. Movie enthusiasts will pay a premium for better quality seats at the cinema. When the value is visible and enhances the overall experience, people are willing to invest more.

Your practice is no different. Everyone wants to feel special and to receive the best service on offer and they're willing to pay more for it. Wherever your pricing structure sits amongst the competition, your customer service must feel like it's the most expensive money can buy! The right patients will come back repeatedly, without fixating on price, when you exceed their expectations.

KAPASiTE

SIMPLIFICATION

Why brevity is key

Whether you're writing content for your website and social media or consulting with a patient for the first time, remember that less is more. I'm talking words! It can be easy to overexplain when talking about your treatments, especially if you're passionate about your work, but the more information you give your patients, the more words there are to take in, the harder it can be to process.

When filmmakers pitch an idea to Hollywood producers, they must come up with a 'logline,' a short sentence or paragraph that sells the idea of the film quickly and efficiently. In business, this is called the elevator pitch. It's a process of taking all the information you have and reducing it to the minimum while still conveying all the necessary information the reader or listener needs to decide.

Where your content and conversations will be longer and more detailed than a logline or elevator pitch, the mechanics are the same. Weed out any information that is surplus or unnecessary at that moment. Keep it succinct and avoid lengthy descriptions or convoluted instructions. Don't use ten words when five will suffice!

We live in a distracted society, and more words than necessary will disengage your patients. They won't say it, but they are thinking it. There is always going to be a patient who wants to talk at length and ask many questions. Of course, you will always be available to answer questions, but the core information should be kept to the point. Patients aren't as passionate about the technology in your practice as you are. Focus on the outcome and how the patient can get there, and leave questions to them. Personally, I can make decisions on very little information because my decision-making pattern begins with trust as a major driving factor.

Keep it simple

You may need to use technical terms when describing your treatments. Be mindful of vocabulary that, although it might be second nature to you, could be wholly intimidating or confusing for patients.

Using simple language makes it easier for patients to understand the information and make informed decisions. Jargon and complex terminology should be minimised. At the same time, it's important not to 'dumb it down' excessively, as patients could perceive such language as condescending. Strive to strike a balance between simplicity and respect for patients' intelligence.

If you find it hard to judge your tone and content, ask someone impartial (who isn't a dentist!) to have a mock consultation with you, they'll be able to give honest feedback on how well you relay your information. You can also use mystery shoppers to receive impartial feedback. **See page 204 on Mystery Shoppers**.

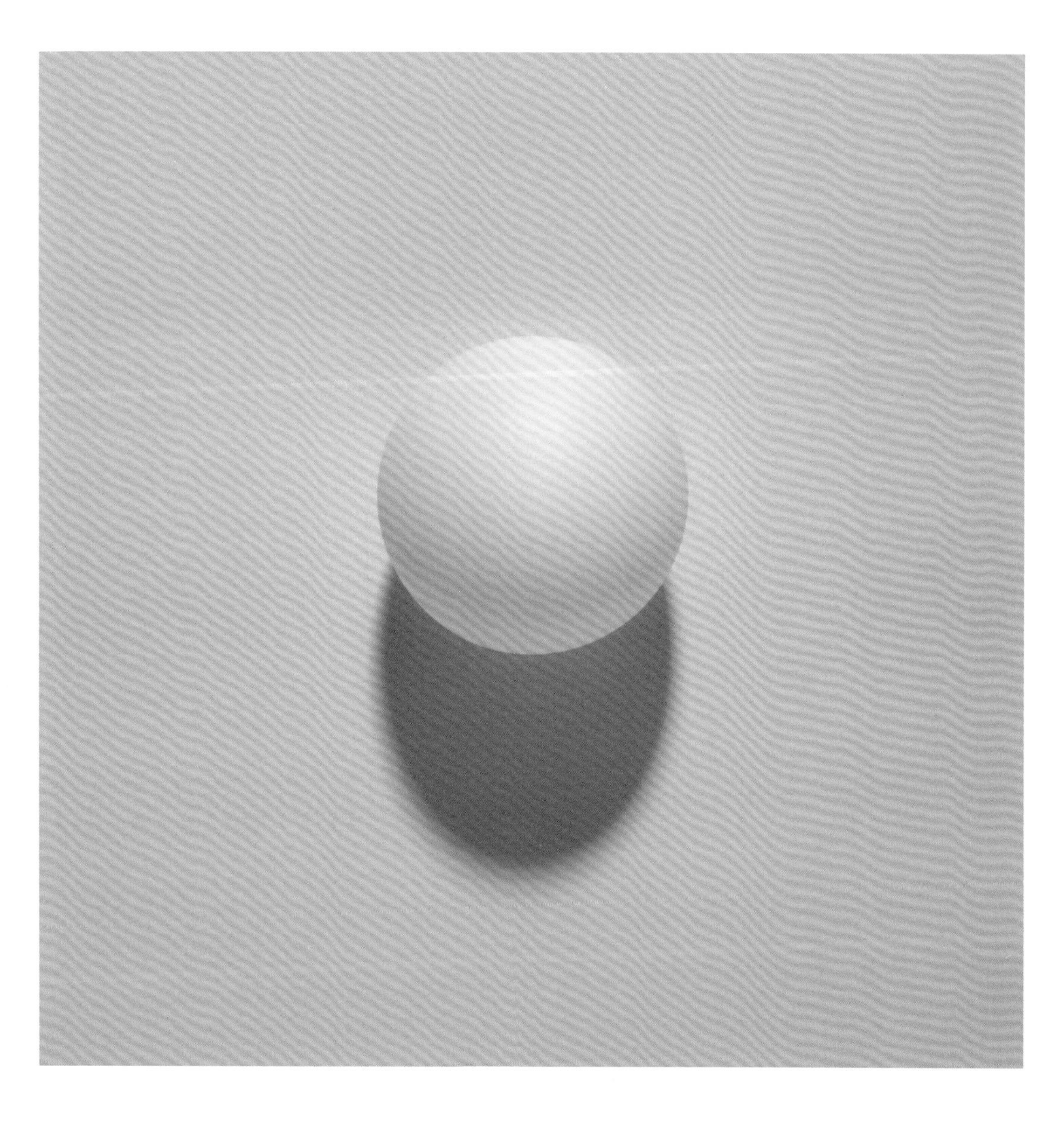

AVENUE
GEORGE V
LOUIS VUITTON

Is your website converting well?

Many people think that customer service begins once you interact with a prospective patient in person, but in truth, it starts much earlier. Ensuring that your brand, practice, and treatments are easily accessible and straightforward to understand is one of the first steps in a patient's journey with you. While branding, imagery and typography are all important aspects of your website, they shouldn't overshadow or come at the expense of the key elements your prospective patients have come looking for.

According to research conducted by my company, Digimax, patients expect certain information to be readily available without clicking or excessive scrolling. Failure to provide this information instantly can result in visitors leaving your site prematurely, or 'bouncing,' as our studies have shown.

The following are some of the most (certainly not all) frequently requested items, and it's important to ensure that they are visible on your website **without having to click or scroll to find them.**

1. Clear address or location at the top of the site
2. Phone number for easy calling
3. Who the practice is catering for specifically
4. Key treatments the practice prides itself in
5. Google reviews for social proof

Speak to my team at Digimax if you need help making your website the most effective for patient conversion. Visit **digimax.dental/contact**

FIRST IMPRESSIONS

OPEN

Lasting first impressions

The importance of first impressions cannot be overstated, in all aspects of life. Research indicates that within the first seven seconds of meeting someone, a strong impression is already established. Once formed, these impressions can be difficult to change. Patients will have already decided whether to trust you and invest their time or money.

To create a positive first impression, always greet anyone (including non-patients) who enters your practice with a warm smile, eye contact, and a friendly welcome. This type of reception should be a consistent feature of your high-level customer service.

It's important to present yourself in a professional and well-groomed manner. While this may seem obvious, the state of your nails, shoes, or hair can all reflect your brand. All staff members should maintain a high standard of personal grooming and presentation. Hotels adhere to an uncompromising gold standard of personal care and grooming. **See page 161 on Looking the part**.

A positive and warm attitude is essential. A polite, cheerful, and upbeat demeanour from your team sets the tone for your patients' visits and makes them feel welcome and valued from the outset. Although it's natural to have off days, it's important not to project negativity onto patients.

Being attentive and taking the time to engage in small talk with patients can help build rapport and trust. Showing an interest in their lives and well-being is an effective way to create a positive and lasting impression.

The 7/11 Rule

Did you know – people make eleven decisions about us in those first seven seconds of contact, known as 'The 7/11 Rule.'

1. Education level
2. Economic level
3. Perceived credibility, believability, competence, and honesty
4. Trustworthiness
5. Level of sophistication
6. Sex role
7. Level of success
8. Political background
9. Religious background
10. Ethnic background
11. Social/professional/sexual desirability

Being aware of the potential impact of these perceptions can help us present our best selves and create a positive and lasting impression on those we meet.

Help plan their visit

You should always be one step ahead of your patients, anticipating their needs and making their experience as stress-free and enjoyable as possible. In doing so, you can give them a sense that you're prepared to go out of your way to accommodate them and that you're doing the thinking for them so that they don't have to!

Sharing your full address, a map, and transport/parking options is a great start and should come as standard for any practice. Think about how you can go above and beyond what they're expecting; for example, highlighting where they can park for free, or paid car parks for longer appointments. Keep your information current – are there roadworks or construction nearby that might impact their journey? Is there a regular Farmers' Market every Monday that will affect their parking options? Knowing what is happening in your local area allows you to help your patients plan their visits with no unexpected issues. Is there a practice nearby that shares a similar name which may confuse patients?

No one likes to arrive stressed or annoyed because of a difficult journey, so by anticipating and addressing any potential obstacles ahead of an appointment, you give them an early insight into the fantastic customer service you'll be delivering. You can also be more direct and ask open-ended questions via email/text messages like 'What can we do to make your visit more comfortable?' letting your patients know that you're already thinking of them before they've even set foot in your practice. **See page 293 on Make giving feedback easy**.

Providing directions

Some patients can get anxious when visiting somewhere new for the first time. I am perpetually early for everything as I hate to get lost and run late, so simple, well-written directions from the local tube, train station, or nearby car parks will be a welcome, added touch to make your patient's visit as easy as possible. Even if your practice is near an underground or train station, a patient may still need help finding you. Providing clear and concise instructions is an absolute must, especially if your competitors are already doing this.

Although I find that you can provide all the information in the world, come an hour before the appointment time, the patient is stressing and churning through emails to find basics such as your address. There is temporary blindness to obvious and key bits of information.

What I like to do is send a text message with a walking directional video an hour before the appointment, as demonstrated in this example I made for attendees of my workshops: **https://shaz.co.uk/walkingdirections**

STAND
ON
THE
RIGHT
Stand on the right
No smoking
Stand on the right

Your local area guide

Receptionists are often the first port of call when someone requires local information, such as the nearest coffee shop, bank, or supermarket. Staff members who know the area well will be able to suggest several options based on their own knowledge and experiences, but your practice can go that extra mile by providing your patients with a professionally designed, printed local area guide, anticipating your patients' questions before they've even asked!

Think about all the different amenities someone might ask about, such as local restaurants, cafes, nearest petrol station, hot-desking spots, nearest cashpoint etc. and make it easy for them to find whatever they need. Include business phone numbers, addresses, and websites. You should also include their distances from your practice or even create a cool local area map to make finding them straightforward.

Be sure to include a few different options under each category. Avoid making personal recommendations, they can backfire! Remember to include your practice name and branding on the guide – your patient's friends and family might see the guide and be blown away at the amount of care and attention you've taken to make your patients' experiences easier and more enjoyable! How many practices are doing this do you think? An easy way to wow.

Pre-appointment pack

Sending a pre-appointment pack to your patients will show how much you care about them before they've even had their first treatment. It's an opportunity for them to get a sense of your brand and your practice and allow you to answer common questions they might have ahead of time. The pack would also contain how they can prepare for the appointment.

Include details about their appointment, such as date and time, how to find you (**See page 68 on Providing directions**), and any other information about the treatment process that may help put them at ease ahead of their visit.

In today's digital age, it may seem counterproductive to send a physical pre-appointment pack to your patients' homes. However, receiving a standout physical item, at the start of treatment, can enhance the patient experience. At Digimax, we call our pre-appointment pack the 'mug box.' We had a high-quality gift box manufactured to impress our enquirers, and it has since become an integral part of our customer service standard operating procedures (SOPs). **See page 194 on Standard operating procedures**.

A nicely presented envelope or package to open to signify the start of their journey can help establish trust and rapport with them from the beginning. You can add even more wow factor by enclosing dental items. Everyone likes an unexpected gift! Plus, like your local area guides, these packs could be seen by other friends or family members in the home, making it a great brand awareness opportunity. It's not unusual to see patients sharing this on social media!

As the saying goes, timing is everything. I always tell my team to send out our mug box by first-class post on the same day we receive the enquiry, so there are increased chances of next-day arrival. There is power in immediacy. Since we send out a lot of mug boxes, we don't typically use a courier service. However, I would recommend using an overnight courier service if you're sending to larger treatment plan patients, including Invisalign. That way, they'll receive an exclusive courier delivery, which adds to the wow factor.

Eye and smile greeting

Perhaps rule one of 5-star hotel standard customer service is to start with a smile.

The power of a smile is undeniable. You don't need me to tell you this. Yet, sometimes as a team, we can forget that they have the power to affect others. Many businesses, particularly in the UK, fail at such a basic part of customer service! Smiling is considered a signal of trustworthiness and intelligence.

Your team training and SOPs should clearly state that every person who enters your premises should be greeted with direct eye contact and a beaming smile, they should immediately be made to feel welcome.

Despite the busy nature of dental practices, it is still possible to maintain a high level of customer service. This has been demonstrated by busy understaffed 5-star hotels around the world, where staff manage to maintain a welcoming smile for every guest, even in the face of numerous challenges. Appearing calm and graceful on the surface while working hard and efficiently underneath, also known as the 'Swan Effect'.

Even if you are on a call or in the middle of another conversation, it's important to acknowledge someone who walks into your practice promptly. Make eye contact, smile, and indicate that you'll be with them as soon as possible. The approach you take may differ depending on the setup and staffing of your practice, but the general rule is to greet patients at the earliest opportunity whenever possible.

Be careful with forced smiles, however. A smile can appear superficial and disingenuous when it doesn't reach the eyes. You must be sincere in your welcome; otherwise, your efforts may have the opposite effect.

The acclaimed spa

My partner and I arrived at a spa we had heard so much about. We stepped through the entrance and saw another guest already engaged in a conversation with the front desk staff. We waited patiently, but in the first 3 minutes we were there, it was as if we were invisible and did not exist. A further 3 minutes must have passed, and now we were 10 minutes away from our appointment time after being advised to be there 15 minutes early to fill in forms. Another few minutes later, the lady behind the front desk greeted us with a smile, apologised for keeping us waiting, and gave us some forms to fill in.

Did they do anything wrong? From typical UK customer service standards level, no! They did exactly what most businesses with a front desk do – made us wait our turn. From 5-star hospitality standards, this was a colossal fail. We came to the spa to relax and unwind, and the experience began the moment we stepped foot in the door: the ambience, smell, and greeting. The lady could have silently signalled to us to let us know she had seen us and would be coming to us soon. Once she noticed that several minutes had passed and we hadn't been seated, she could have even politely asked permission from her current guest to speak with us and very quickly briefed us that she wouldn't be much longer.

If patients have questions, doubts, or worries from the moment they enter your premises – that is not a great start! This may sound like a hyper-analysis of a normal daily situation – however, these very situations allow us to pull out our wow cards and build patients for life!

Give patients a tour of your facilities

The easiest wow win: Instead of leaving patients to figure out the facilities on their own, take the initiative to introduce them.

Rather than simply directing them to your lounge (a.k.a waiting area), taking the time to give patients a tour of your clinic will make them feel welcomed and valued. Arriving for an appointment can be nerve-wracking, so putting them at ease from the moment they enter your door is important. Additionally, introducing them to key areas, such as the washroom and refreshment stations, can make their experience more comfortable and stress-free.

Streamline your patient's experience by anticipating their needs.

Keep spaces clutter-free

It goes without saying that a clinical environment such as your dental practice should be fastidiously clean, but tidiness is just as important. Unnecessary clutter can overshadow the feeling of cleanliness. Your waiting area may be messy, and you don't see it because it's a familiar space.

Where possible, minimise (if not eradicate) irrelevant leaflet displays, posters, stacks of magazines, and overall unnecessary visual noise in the practice. Make sure personal belongings are stored out of sight and keep your reception area free from visible food or drink. The most sophisticated settings are minimal.

The saying 'tidy desk, tidy mind' applies to larger areas too! Clutter-free, open spaces offer a serene and organised setting for your patients.

Less is certainly more!

Invest in nice smells

Smell is the most evocative of the senses. Closely linked with memory, what we smell can affect our mood and emotions; certain scents release oxytocin, the 'happy' hormone.

Smells can also evoke negative feelings – many people dislike the smell of hospitals. The clinical, medical smell can be off-putting for some; for others, the smell may recall memories of less happy moments, after all, hospitals aren't exactly known for fun times. Just because your practice is a clinical setting doesn't mean it should smell as such. When your patients walk through the door, the smell will be one of the first things they notice before any of the other senses have had time to take everything in.

Introducing a fragrant and natural aroma through flowers can be a delightful experience. Additionally, you may explore the use of high-quality essential oil diffusers, plug-ins, or scented sticks. Certain fragrances and reputable brands like Jo Malone, Neom, and the White Company are synonymous with quality. Your patients will recognise the captivating fragrance as a symbol of sophistication, establishing a positive association between your brand and discerning preferences.

Be considerate of personal scents. When engaging in treatments that necessitate close contact with patients, it's important to avoid overwhelming them with strong perfumes or aftershaves. I recall a particular incident during a flight where an air hostess would pass by, enveloping me in an overpowering oud fragrance that made it difficult to breathe. Such experiences can be uncomfortable and should be avoided in order to ensure a pleasant environment for everyone involved.

Clinic aesthetics

When viewing your practice through fresh eyes, what do you see? Does it exude a warm and inviting atmosphere? Are the reception and waiting areas visually appealing and comfortable? A patient's first impression is important, and upon entering your practice, they may notice any signs of wear and tear such as scuffed seating, damaged walls, worn floors, or a general lack of upkeep, leading to unfair assumptions of the overall standards of your practice.

It's important to ensure that your practice's aesthetics reflect your brand and make your patients feel at ease. For instance, a luxury practice in a high-needs NHS setting may make patients uncomfortable, just as basic blue chairs in the patient lounge and dated tube lighting in a high-end practice setting could damage your brand perception.

When in doubt, simplicity and minimalism can go a long way. Your practice's interior doesn't necessarily need to be luxurious. Brands like Marks and Spencer and John Lewis provide great examples of brands that cater to all types of shoppers. Consider taking a similar approach if you are a mixed high-quality practice. Remember, the little details matter and can make a big impact on how patients perceive your practice.

Tuning into wellness

Playing music in your reception and treatment rooms has the potential to completely transform a person's feelings towards an environment, helping them to feel more relaxed, so consider some neutrally tasteful tunes for a calming background ambience. Everyone has different music tastes, so avoid anything too genre-specific or loud. I suggest avoiding playing Heart FM as you don't want to sound like a barber shop or an Uber (No offence barbers and Uber drivers)!

Refreshments on arrival

We all love an excellent level of hospitality wherever we go, so offer your patients a refreshment on arrival and aim to have a good selection.

If a patient expresses a preference for something you don't have, make a note of it so that you can offer it next time. **See page 121 on Drink preferences**.

Introduce

Front-of-house team members should introduce themselves, assure the patients of a comfortable experience, and ask them if they need anything to make their experience more pleasant.

How you greet your patients should be consistent, for all team members, at all times. Having a service manual for your practice with information on how patients should be welcomed is a great way of keeping things consistent. **See page 190 on Customer service manual.**

Keep your patients connected

I'm sure that at one point or another, everyone has experienced that heart-sinking feeling of their phone battery dying when out and about with nowhere to charge it. So many of us use our phones to stay constantly connected that a dead battery can cause a great deal of anxiety, especially for parents.

During an Uber ride, I was pleasantly surprised when the driver offered me an all-in-one charger with multiple phone leads. He went the extra mile in customer service by anticipating my needs and asking if I would like to charge my phone. This level of service exceeded my expectations and earned him a 5-star rating.

Provide the same high level of service for your patients and keep a selection of phone chargers in your reception for just these occasions, and when possible, design your waiting room to allow easy access to a charging point so that your patients can keep their phones in their possession while charging.

Providing the Wi-Fi password without patients needing to ask is another way to keep your patients happy and connected. You can print out the password onto a card and hand it to your patients, just like they do in leading hotels, so your patients do not have to come up and ask you themselves. Plus, the easier it is for patients to be online, the easier it is for them to tag you in any social media posts!

LOVE TEETH
DENTAL PRACTICE
Dr.
KP

Calling next: Love Teeth's way

In their rapidly expanding dental practice, Love Teeth Dental, Kunal and Lucy Patel passionately prioritise patient experience and take customer service to the next level. Lucy hates the impersonal atmosphere that often permeates typical medical waiting rooms. She laments situations where patients' names are called out into the void, where the person behind the name remains a mystery until they stand up and make themselves known.

To counter this, Love Teeth Dental has implemented a uniquely personalised approach. Their front-of-house team is trained to guide each patient to a specific chair in the waiting room, cleverly numbered in their internal system. This allows the dentist to stride directly to the patient when it's their turn, greeting them personally rather than merely calling out a name.

Such a detail might seem insignificant, and indeed it could even slip past unnoticed by some. However, when combined with the other fifty-plus modifications that the Patels have made to enhance the patient experience, its impact becomes clearer. These collective efforts significantly boost their reputation, fuel practice growth, and create a positive vibe among the team, especially when they attract the type of patients they prefer to serve.

Patients who have multiple consultations often lean towards Love Teeth Dental, even though their prices may not be the lowest. This is because the practice's meticulous attention to seemingly small details sets an expectation for the quality of care to come. The consistent delivery on this promise is what sets Love Teeth Dental apart. The Patels' dedication to personalising the dental experience is commendable. Well done, Love Teeth.

THE VIP TREATMENT

BUSINESS CLA

Personalise auto replies

According to a study conducted by the *Harvard Business Review*, businesses that respond to customer enquiries within an hour are nearly seven times more likely to qualify the lead than those who respond an hour later. The study analysed over 1.25 million leads across multiple industries and found that the odds of making a successful connection with a lead decreasing by over 10 times in the first hour. This emphasises the importance of a quick response time in lead conversion and customer acquisition.

Whilst it might sound obvious to reply as quickly as possible, many practices aren't obsessive about responding back to patients as fast as possible. The above study demonstrates just how important speedy responses are.

Ensure your email address is sending an enthusiastic auto reply to the patient informing them of the next steps and assuring them the email will be responded to within a short and specific time frame. This is a promise you must keep! Make this email stand out and add in a lot of enthusiasm. The next page will explain why this simple enquiry is a critical moment in the patient's journey. Usually, the patient has gone through five stages before reaching the enquiry stage.

A buyer's journey

The mindset stages of a patient when enquiring with a practice can vary depending on the individual and their specific situation, but generally, they follow a similar pattern.

1. **Awareness**: The patient becomes aware of a need or desire for a particular treatment
2. **Consideration**: The patient begins to research and consider different options that are available to them
3. **Intent**: The patient decides to take action and actively looks for a solution that meets their needs
4. **Evaluation**: The patient evaluates the available options and decides which one to choose
5. **Purchase**: The patient makes a purchase decision and either makes a purchase or schedules an appointment
6. **Post-purchase**: After the appointment or treatment, the patient evaluates their experience and decides whether to continue

First names enhance interactions

Using someone's name increases likeability and rapport between individuals, according to a study published in the journal *Social Influence*. Researchers found that participants who were addressed by their names during a conversation rated the interaction more positively and had a higher level of rapport with the person they were talking to. Additionally, a study published in the Journal of *Personality and Social Psychology* found that using someone's name can increase their engagement and attention in a conversation. Researchers found that participants were more likely to respond to questions and had a higher level of social involvement when their names were used during the conversation.

You should always address your patients by their first name, it shows that you don't simply view them as another patient or as a transaction but as an individual with their own unique needs and expectations. It also conveys an element of competency and respect. Your patients will know that you interact with multiple people in a day, so the fact that you remember their name will make them feel important and validated.

If you're not sure how to pronounce a name, ask! For years I had only seen the name 'Siobhan' written down. I had no idea it was pronounced 'Shi-Vawhn' If you have a patient with a hard-to-pronounce name, make a note of how to say it and put the phonetic pronunciation in their patient preferences so that your colleagues are informed. Your patients will be wowed if a member of staff they haven't met before gets their name right first time – especially if their name is Aoife or Saoirse!

Bonjour, hola, hello

It's highly likely that you have patients who are not native English speakers and may encounter difficulties with the language. Having members of staff who speak different languages is always a fantastic way to build rapport, but even if you don't, learning how to greet someone in a foreign language is a small but effective touch to make a patient feel warmly welcomed.

Consider including a reference in your patient notes regarding how to greet your patients in their mother tongue, and don't worry if you say it slightly wrong the first time; most patients will just be happy that you've made an effort and will be glad to teach you the proper pronunciation.

辣條伍包
壹角
人民供銷

Cultural diversity

It is a common misconception to think that 'welcome' is simply the initial process of greeting a patient on arrival; it is so much more than that. It is the overall attitude of team members towards patients at any given time for the duration of their time with you.

Being aware of cultural differences can go a long way toward making a patient feel relaxed and at ease.

British people are often perceived as slightly more reserved than many cultures, so a firm handshake greeting with eye contact is standard. However, when shaking hands with someone from China, they prefer a lighter handshake and no eye contact. Many Muslims believe that physical contact with the opposite sex is unnecessary, discouraged, and for some, even prohibited. So, for a male member of staff greeting a Muslim headscarf-wearing female patient, a smile will suffice.

Everyone will be different, but being aware of cultural differences and noting how your patients like to be greeted shows enormous respect for them and their culture. This is a vital part of hospitality training in leading hotels.

Non-verbal communication

It's important to note that nonverbal communication isn't just about what we want to convey, but also about what we may be unconsciously communicating. Some team members may display their personal problems through their nonverbal communication, such as slouching, avoiding eye contact, or appearing disinterested. It's important to address these issues and provide valuable and meaningful support to those team members. At the same time, it's crucial to recognise that this aura can be contagious and affect the team's overall morale and patient experience.

One way to combat this is to foster a positive and supportive work environment where team members feel comfortable sharing their struggles and seeking help when needed. Regular check-ins, team-building activities, and open communication channels can help to create a supportive culture where team members feel valued and heard.

Positive nonverbal cues such as smiling, making eye contact, and using open body language can help to create a welcoming and reassuring environment for patients. These small gestures can go a long way in building rapport and trust with patients and can make a big difference in their overall experience at your practice.

By being mindful of our body language, facial expressions, and other nonverbal cues, we can create a more positive and welcoming environment for our patients. Additionally, by addressing any negative nonverbal communication among team members, we can create a supportive and positive workplace culture that benefits everyone.

Body language

We learn to read body language from a young age, generally from upsetting our parents! That raised eyebrow with crossed arms from a parent would be enough to know you are in deep trouble!

As an adult, reading body language is an integral part of communicating in both our personal and business lives and being able to read your patient's body language will help you provide a better customer experience. Tailoring communication to individual interactions is essential; a universal approach in face-to-face interactions falls short.

We can all read facial expressions, we can usually tell if someone is happy, sad, or angry, but there are many other tell-tale signs to let you know if your patient is comfortable. Rapid blinking, nail-biting, or fidgeting can all represent nervousness or anxiety. Pursed lips, crossed arms, or foot tapping can express impatience or annoyance.

A patient might be too shy to let you know that they are nervous about a treatment, but if you can read their subtle, non-verbal signs of anxiety, you can make them feel more at ease. Likewise, if you see that they are unhappy about something, you can anticipate a potential complaint and address it accordingly before they have to say anything.

Remember, reading body language goes both ways. If you are unsmiling, stiff, or lost in your thoughts, your patients will pick up on this. Some of us have a natural resting face that looks downbeat or annoyed. If this sounds like you, try to be conscious of this when you're with your patients, make the effort to smile, and 'open up' your face to be friendlier and more welcoming.

Body language and their meanings

I have included this table to help with your team training. It's important to note that these gestures can have different meanings in different contexts and that nonverbal communication should always be interpreted in conjunction with verbal communication and the overall situation. However, being aware of negative body language and addressing it can help to improve communication and build better relationships with patients.

Gesture	Meaning
Crossed arms	Defensive, closed-off, disengaged
Frowning	Disapproval, unhappiness, anger
Slouching	Laziness, lack of confidence, disinterest
Avoiding eye contact	Dishonesty, shyness, lack of interest
Excessive fidgeting	Nervousness, discomfort, boredom
Tapping foot	Impatience, annoyance, frustration
Rolled eyes	Disrespect, boredom, exasperation
Standing too close	Aggressiveness, invading personal space
Clenched fists	Anger, aggression, defensiveness
Arms on hips	Defiance, impatience, confrontational
Playing with hair	Nervousness, discomfort, insecurity
Looking at watch frequently	Impatience, boredom, lack of interest

Patient preferences with profile notes

Leading hotels use 'profile notes' to provide personalised service to their guests. These notes contain information about the guest's preferences, which enables the staff to deliver a quality service that keeps their guests returning to the property. This concept of profile notes isn't limited to hotels; dental practices can implement their own system to log their patients' preferences. As team members get to know their patients, they can make a note of their likes and dislikes. For example, they can note down their favourite drinks, preferred choice of music, names of significant people in their life, or upcoming special occasions or holidays.

By creating and maintaining these profile notes, all team members can access them and proactively act on them. They can use this information to provide a more personalised experience for the patient, including small personal touches that can turn into a wow moment. This demonstrates that the team is thoughtful and always looking to exceed the patient's expectations. Such a personal touch will make the patients feel valued and cared for and are more likely to return and recommend the practice to others. The key is to be consistent in maintaining these notes and acting on them, which can lead to a higher level of patient satisfaction and a more thriving dental practice.

For example, if a patient shares that they are going on a holiday to a particular destination for the first time, there are several things you can do with this information to enhance their experience and leave a lasting impression:

- Send them a city guide with a personalised note via Amazon
- Ask about their trip on their next visit to the practice
- Inform front of house to ask about the patient's trip on their next visit
- Mention their upcoming break in written communications both pre- and post- trip

You have the power to create a patient experience that will stay with them for a lifetime and have them singing your praises to everyone they know. Take the time to get to know your patients and find ways to make their experience unforgettable.

52891
34741

13°C

Temperature preferences

The temperature of a room can make all the difference to whether a person feels comfortable and at ease, particularly in a healthcare setting. Everyone has different comfort levels regarding heat and cold; that's why my postman wears shorts all year round while I'm digging out my winter clothes in September!

Many patients may not mention if they're feeling too cold or warm, so you should ask them outright if they're comfortable and if they'd like you to adjust the heating or air conditioning. Assure them that it's no trouble at all to adjust the temperature, since the default answer is often 'it's fine,' and only after a little prodding might someone open up.

Another idea is to ask patients about their temperature preferences before they arrive, perhaps through a questionnaire. For example, you could ask 'Please specify your room temperature preference' on a form, which could help you prepare the room and ensure that the patient feels comfortable as soon as they arrive.

Music preferences

Music has a positive effect on reducing anxiety and stress. Studies have demonstrated that music can lower biological stress responses such as heart rate and cortisol levels.

In addition to having music in your patient lounge, you can take patient experience to the next level by knowing their music preferences before an appointment. Imagine their delight when they hear their favourite artist or music is playing in your treatment room when they arrive. It shows that you care about their preferences and have taken the time to create a personalised experience for them. This can also help them feel more relaxed and at ease, leading to a more enjoyable treatment experience. By going the extra mile to cater to their preferences, your patients are more likely to remember your practice and share their positive experience with others.

FILTER COFFEE
ESPRESSO
SINGLE ORIGIN COFFEE
MACCHIATO
ONE AND ONE
CAPPUCCINO
LATTE
MOCHA
CHAI

Drink preferences

Remembering what your patients like to drink and offering it to them on arrival is a great way to create a wow moment.

Share a menu with patients before arrival that they can digitally select so their drink is waiting for them. Not many businesses are doing this! Give patients a reason to talk about you.

Make the menu interesting, though be careful not to provide options that could backfire due to complex preferences. The drinks should be easy to prepare.

Exceptional customer service is not just about providing a one-off positive experience, but about setting a standard for your practice. To maintain this standard, it is essential to have systems and infrastructure in place to ensure that your patients receive what they ordered and expect.

By paying attention to the small details and putting in place procedures to ensure accuracy, you can provide exceptional customer service consistently.

The case of the awkward protein shakes

As Rachel the Principal Dentist, walked into the practice each day with her trusty protein shake in hand, she never expected that her routine would catch the attention of a new team member. This observant individual took notice and decided to act.

Approaching Rachel one day, the team member said, 'I noticed you have a particular brand of protein shake. To save you time and ensure you get a cold one each morning, I have bought a case and kept them in the fridge for you.'

Rachel was blown away by the thoughtful gesture. She felt seen and appreciated. However, as she opened the fridge to grab her shake the next day, she realised something was off. The flavour was not what she was accustomed to. Instead of her beloved regular chocolate, she was faced with an unknown flavour that tasted like toxic waste.

Confused and unsure of how to proceed, Rachel found herself in a difficult situation. She didn't want to hurt the team member's feelings, as they had put in so much effort to anticipate her needs. At the same time, she had an awkward situation on her hands.

This experience taught Rachel a valuable lesson: if you're going to anticipate someone's needs, you must get the details right. Even the smallest oversight can cause the entire effort to backfire.

Make sure you pay attention to the details. It's the little things that make all the difference in providing exceptional customer service.

Remember birthdays and special occasions

As children we LOVE our birthday, but as we get older, it's not quite the same as when we are young. We may not get as many presents for a start! Also, nowadays, we usually get birthday wishes on social media instead of a card, so when someone takes the time to send a handwritten birthday card that arrives in time for your actual birthday, it makes it much more special. It shows that they cared enough to remember and didn't need to be reminded by social media on the day.

Use the date of birth information on file to send your patients birthday cards. Have a graphic designer create a range of custom-designed birthday cards to ensure a patient doesn't receive the same card design twice. Ask a staff member with the neatest handwriting to write in the card and get the whole team to sign it. Sending a birthday card is a simple and inexpensive way to put a smile on your patient's face.

You could also have cards made for special occasions, e.g., the birth of a new-born, 'Congratulations' and 'Get Well Soon' cards. Take the time to listen to what patients share with you about their lives and create a real wow moment by sending them your best wishes for that upcoming anniversary they mentioned – or the exam they recently passed. At Digimax, we have 14 different types of greeting cards, and we send almost 2000 of these out every year.

Remember important moments

I went to one of my favourite restaurants a while ago, and the waiter asked me how my house move went. Embarrassingly, I didn't even remember telling him, but I was pleasantly surprised that not only did he remember me, but our conversation too.

If your patients mention important moments in their lives, make a note! Perhaps their son's or daughter's exams are on, or they have a big anniversary coming up. It might be something small but significant that you can mention on their next visit, or for something bigger, consider sending a card and/or a gift. When you remember these important moments, you make your patients feel important and valued.

Taken from Mt Nelson
Mr. Bailey in background
Jan 17 1915.
Oh how I wish you had
of been with us!

POST CARD.

THIS SIDE FOR CORRESPONDENCE

Dec. 31st 1915
Dear friend I reached
home safe but I am
feeling very lonely
I miss you so much
look for letter soon
pleasant dreams be
yours M.A.A.

THE ADDRESS TO BE W[...]
ON THIS SID[...]

NORFOLK AND [...]
TRA
JAN
1
1916

C. E. Lea
R.#1 Box 30
Blanche N.C.

Remember important people

We all have important people in our lives, significant others, family, and children. When you take the time to remember these people and ask after them, it shows care for your patients, telling them that their lives and loved ones are important to you too.

Take note of the names and other personal details that patients mention during their visits. Perhaps they mentioned that their children are starting a new school or that their spouse got a promotion. These seemingly small notes can make a big difference in building strong patient relationships and enhancing their experience at your practice.

5-star email etiquette

With emails flooding our inboxes more than ever, it's vital to utilise a collection of pre-written emails designed by you that can be personalised to fit any situation. This guarantees a consistent standard of communication, much like what's seen in leading hotels. Writing personalised emails, backed by a proven format, that are both enthusiastic and distinct, can create a memorable and positive experience for the patient.

By changing a few words, we can elevate a brand experience over email:

Instead of	Say
Hi John	Good Morning / Afternoon / Evening John
I hope this email finds you well	I hope you are having a fantastic day! [Add some personalisation about the weather, neutral current events, or something you know about the recipient's schedule (upcoming holiday / house move / newborn)
Thanks	Of course, if I can be of any further assistance, please do not hesitate to reach out! Thank you.
Yes we can do that	Absolutely, we can certainly do that for you!
Let me check	That is a great question, I am going to find out and come right back to you!
See you soon	We look forward to meeting you! We look forward to seeing you! We can't wait to meet you! We are excited to meet you! We are so excited to welcome you to our practice!
Absence of reassurance	Our practice is designed around the comfort of our patients. Please do let me know if you need assistance with any information before your arrival or if you have any special requests! We will always do our best to accommodate!
Absence of gratitude	We are so grateful for your custom! It means so much to us!

Powerful service phrases

Instead of	What a patient heard / felt	Say
Sir/Madam	You don't know my name	Always use last name with title (e.g.: Mr. Rogers)
Hi, Hello	This is how you greet friends & family. It's an informal greeting	Always use last name with title (e.g.: Mr. Rogers)
Uh-huh, Okay	Gives the feeling that we are uninterested or can't be bothered	I see, Perfect, Of course, Certainly, Absolutely
You should have... Why didn't you...	Makes patients feel like we are blaming them	May I ask if you...?
You have to...	Makes patients feel like they are being forced to do something	Would you mind....
Have a good day	Indifferent feeling	Have an amazing day. You can use alternative words to replace amazing: Incredible / Brilliant / Excellent / Fabulous / Fantastic / Great / Marvellous / Magnificent Outstanding / Perfect / Superb / Spectacular / Wonderful
'Good' in response to a question about your day	Gives the feeling that we don't enjoy our job	My day has been super! Thank you so much for asking. Replace 'super' with alternative words as above.

Instead of	What a patient heard / felt	Say
I will try to get that to you	If we can be bothered, we will get that to you	Certainly, I will arrange that for you
That's impossible	Is aggressive and shows the patient a lack of effort	What I can offer you is What I can do for you is
As soon as possible (ASAP)	That doesn't tell me much	Let's be specific: It will arrive in 10 minutes I will get this to you by 3pm I will come back to you by 3pm This will be completed by 4pm
I am only a receptionist. I am just a receptionist and that is not my department.	We should never devalue ourselves. We all represent the company so lets be positive in our response	I will make sure that my manager is aware of this matter I will look into this for you
It's not my job	In the patient's mind it is our job	Please tell me how I can be of assistance?
It's your fault	Aggressive and places blame	I can see that you are disappointed. Could you tell me exactly what happened?
You're confusing me	We are blaming the patient	Would you be kind enough to share with me exactly what happened please? Ask more questions related to the topic

Instead of	What a patient heard / felt	Say
Who told you that? Who said that?	Disorganised	There seems to be a misunderstanding. Would you be kind enough to share what happened?
It's company policy	Rigid	The reason for this is ...... I really want to assist you with this situation. How would you think we could reach an agreement?
Ah, where is my head at, my mistake!	This company makes mistakes!	Please accept my sincerest apologies. Let me take care of this for you.
Cheap	Low quality brand	Inexepensive
I can't do that	Shows a lack of effort	What I can do for you is...
I don't know	Shows a lack of effort	Good question, let me check and find that out for you.
No	Shows a lack of effort	Unfortunately, I am not able to do that, but I can...
Are you sure?	Does she think I am stupid?	That's most unusual. Would you be kind enough to tell me exactly what happened?

Email examples

Lacklustre email example	Alternative '5-star' response
Hi John, I will check and come back to you. Cheers Richard Smith	Dear Mr. Simpson, I hope you are well and having a fantastic day so far! (On a Monday or return from a bank holiday: I hope you are well and had a fantastic weekend!) (Also, use Wonderful, Lovely, Great, Enjoyable, Restful replacing 'Fantastic' and mixing things up) That is a fantastic question. [Insert answer here] I hope this answers your question. Of course, if you have any further questions, please do not hesitate to get back in touch. Best wishes Your name
Hello John, Thanks for your email. I have received your email and will be in touch. Your name	Dear Mr. Simpson, Thank you for your email relating to [topic or request]. I just wanted to let you know I have received your email and I will be responding to you shortly. Of course, in the meantime, if you need anything else, please do not hesitate to contact me. Best wishes Your name

Lacklustre email example	Alternative '5-star' response
John, I will investigate this matter and come back to you. Your name	Dear Mr. Simpson, Thank you for raising your concerns / experience about [insert topic / complaint area]. I am sorry to hear about your experience! I am investigating this as a matter of priority. Thank you so much for bringing this to our attention. Please could you help me understand by clarifying [insert specific questions] so that I may best assist you. Alternatively, if you would prefer that we call you, please do let me know the time and date options and best telephone number to reach you on. Of course, in the meantime, if you need anything else, please do not hesitate to contact me. Best wishes Your name

Exceed expectations

I talked about **Emphasis on exceeding on page 33**, but it is such an integral part of customer service that I'm going to talk about it again. The most successful businesses are those that go above and beyond what the customer is expecting.

Think about how you could do it even better in everything you do. Put yourself in your patient's position; what would make you go wow? What can you do to step up and exceed their expectations?

Great customer service will become second nature if your mindset is based around exceeding. Maybe create a reward system for team members that bring ideas to you that can be implemented.

At the end of each year at Digimax, we reflect on all the new client experience changes we made, however small. Every move, has a compound effect.

Target and the interview

Interviews can be stressful enough without being properly attired! In 2014, a young man from North Carolina was on his way to an interview. He stopped at his local Target store and asked an employee for help finding a clip-on tie; unfortunately, Target only sold regular ties.

Rather than shrug his shoulders, the Target employee offered to show the young man how to tie a tie. He even helped practice some handshakes and went through some mock interview questions.

When the young man went to leave, the rest of the Target employees gave him a loud cheer and wished him luck. Another shopper in the store captured the interaction and uploaded it to Facebook.

Not only did the Target employee show real empathy and a genuine desire to help, but the whole team also came together to help make that young man feel great ahead of his interview.

Being genuine, treating everyone with respect, and exceeding the customers' expectations, whether someone is filming you or not, is what makes excellent customer service stand out.

Remove the grit

When we are so focussed on providing wow moments for our patients, it can be easy to overlook the minor annoyances or glitches they encounter when doing business with us. Small grievances like not explaining why they must complete a form that they have completed previously, typos in a patient's name, or not being advised of roadworks that affect their parking are small details in the grand scheme of things, but these are the little things that get tattooed on a patient's mind when they think about their experience.

Have you ever been in a rush to get somewhere, and you had a little stone in your shoe, but it wasn't annoying enough to stop and sort it out? It didn't stop you from reaching your destination, but I have no doubt it wasn't pleasant.

Remove that stone from your patient's journeys! Take away the grit and frustrations. Don't be afraid to ask your patients directly if there is anything about their experience that they find annoying, and work with your team to identify any recurring issues, no matter how small or seemingly insignificant.

Make sure to read all feedback forms and surveys thoroughly. You may find that multiple patients mention the same small grievance, which should be acted upon and fixed as quickly as possible.

At Digimax, if I hear something more than once that needs attention, we make a system for it right away. You can imagine how many of these systems we have built over 20 years!

Eradicate inconveniences

Nobody likes to be inconvenienced. It's annoying, can be time-consuming, and casts a shadow on our day. A great customer experience flows smoothly, is hassle-free, and takes up as little of our time as possible.

During the pandemic, I had to book a Covid test. I filled out a (very) long personal details form online and went through the payment process. When I arrived for my appointment, the receptionist handed me the same form to fill out again. When I queried this, she shrugged and said that was what she was taught to do. It was a minor inconvenience to me in the grand scheme of things, but one that certainly coloured my judgment of the testing provider. Better systems in place and a better attitude would have been an easy and simple fix.

Ensure that all internal systems are as simple as possible for your patients to save time and annoyance. Review your standard operating procedures regularly to see where you can streamline any processes. Ask for feedback on how you could have done things better. Don't assume that in the absence of complaints, that there is no reason to review the most basic elements of your patient experience.

We don't always have control over outside inconveniences, such as train strikes or traffic, but how we deal with them can make all the difference. When you are aware of external circumstances that may inconvenience your patient, you should be proactive by looking at ways to make things easier for them. Let them know if there are roadworks or road closures in your local area or provide them with alternative transport options if there are train strikes.

Make every step of your patient's journey with you as simple and convenient as possible.

Moments of truth

Moments of truth are what every business works towards—the ultimate delivery. When we book a hotel room online, the moment of truth is when we open the door for the very first time. At a restaurant, it is that first mouthful of food; for a wedding photographer, it is showing the bride and groom their pictures for the first time.

The big smile reveal could be the moment of truth in your patient's journey. Ultimately, the most critical part of the experience is fulfilling the promise you've made, and this happens when your patient's moment of truth arrives.

Being aware of your patient's moment of truth is a crucial step in providing exceptional customer service. Take this opportunity to make their experience truly special. Consider how you can enhance this pivotal moment for the patient. Seeing their new smile for the first time is an exciting day, so think of ways to commemorate the occasion and set the tone for how they rave about you later on.

The five moments of truth

The idea of 'moments of truth' began with A.G. Lafley, Chairman, President, and CEO of Procter & Gamble, in 2005. He initially outlined just two moments, but with the introduction of smartphones and social media, these expanded to five different moments of truth to truly reflect the modern customer journey.

<ZMOT: Less than zero moment of truth

This is the very beginning of your patient journey. The first time they know about you and their initial interest. This is an opportunity to be proactive and reach out to prospective patients before they've even begun to research or ask questions of their own.

ZMOT: Zero moment of truth

This moment of truth is when patients begin searching for information about you. Often this will be done online, and so an incredible website, pro-active social media and positive reviews that enhance your reputation will encourage patients to take the next step of their journey with you.

FMOT: First moment of truth

This first moment of truth is based on the moment a patient encounters your treatments for the first time. This could be from reading about you or hearing a recommendation. It might only be a brief moment, but the impression they get in those few seconds can make all the difference to whether they choose to continue learning about you or not.

SMOT: Second moment of truth

A patient making an enquiry for the very first time, or even having a consultation with you, is your second moment of truth. They have not yet committed or booked, so this moment will have a great influence on whether a patient decides whether to pay for a treatment with you.

UMOT: Ultimate moment of truth

Also known as the third moment of truth, this could be your smile reveal. This is the part of your patients journey where they respond to the whole experience to date, culminating in the final delivery. It will shape their emotional response to the service they have received and influence what they say about you and who they tell.

Pre-schedule after-care call

Excellent customer service doesn't end with a smile reveal. It should be an ongoing process, and your practice philosophy should be to make your patients feel valued and cared for long after their final treatment.

If your attention to your patients ends as soon as their treatments are finished, you reduce them to a transaction. You will make them feel as though they were only important while they were spending money. Provide a high level of customer service, even after they've left your practice, and arrange a time where you can call to check in with them after their treatment.

Most patients will appreciate an aftercare call. It also gives them a chance to ask any questions or raise any concerns they might have.

Not only does this show that their well-being is important to you, but it also offers the opportunity to get feedback on how your patient found their experience. Some people may find it easier to be honest and open about their feelings when they are not doing so in person.

Every patient is a walking and talking advertisement for your practice. Proactively address any concerns a patient might have and exceed their expectations by showing that you genuinely care. This approach reduces the risk that a patient will not speak about you with their friends simply because their experience was 'good' but not 'great' enough to rave about.

The art of presenting water

At my agency Digimax, we understand that even seemingly insignificant details can leave a lasting impression on our guests. That's why we have a standardised operating procedure (SOP) for presenting a glass of water. While it might seem unusual or over-the-top at first, it's these small touches that elevate our service and are a reflection of our commitment to excellence.

Consistency is a cornerstone of our customer service philosophy. By adhering to our SOP, we aim to create a familiar and seamless experience for all our guests.

Standard Operating Procedure (SOP) – Serving water to a guest:

1. 10 minutes before any meeting or guest arrival, check the schedule to determine the number of guests attending. Retrieve the appropriate number of Digimax glasses from the kitchen cabinet labelled 'Glassware.' In case of uncertainty about the guest count, take an extra glass as a backup.
2. Examine the glass for streaks, smudges, or any signs of dirt. If the glass is not clean and streak-free (Follow SOP: Cleaning a glass).
3. Utilise the water dispenser to fill the glass, ensuring that the water level reaches the tip of the D symbol on the glass.
4. Place a drink placemat on the desk where the meeting will occur. Align the placemat neatly and level it with any other placemats being placed on the desk.
5. Position the glass in front of the guest's designated seat, ensuring that the D symbol on the glass faces the guest.
6. As your guest arrives, extend a warm greeting (Follow SOP: Greeting guests). Politely offer other beverage choices (Follow SOP: Offering guests drinks).

Remember, the little things matter, and our commitment to providing exceptional service starts with a glass of water. **See page 194 on Standard operating procedures.**

NO TIME
FOR
FAKE PEOPLE

BUILDING A GREAT TEAM

Teamwork makes the dream work

Henry Ford once said, 'If everyone is moving forward together, then success takes care of itself'.

The power of teamwork is undeniable. When individuals work together, they can accomplish more than they could ever achieve alone. In his book *Good to Great*, author Jim Collins highlights the importance of building a strong team as a key factor in achieving business success. Collins argues that the most successful companies are those that focus on finding and retaining the right people and then creating a culture of collaboration and shared purpose.

One of the key lessons from *Good to Great* is the importance of getting the right people on the bus. Collins argues that successful companies start by identifying the right individuals for their team and then creating an environment in which these individuals can thrive. This means not only finding people with the necessary skills and experience, but also individuals who share the company's values and vision. By creating a team of like-minded individuals who are committed to a common purpose, companies can create a culture of collaboration and teamwork that drives success.

Another important lesson from *Good to Great* is the need for leaders to create a culture of discipline. This means establishing clear goals and expectations, setting up systems and processes to support these goals, and holding everyone accountable for their actions. When everyone on the team is aligned around a common goal and understands their role in achieving it, they are more likely to work together to overcome challenges and achieve success. By creating a culture of discipline, companies can build a team that is focused, motivated, and committed to achieving its goals.

Look the part

Personal appearance is a crucial element in the hospitality sector, as it plays a significant role in creating a positive impression on guests. Studies have shown that people form an opinion of someone within seconds of meeting them, and personal appearance is a significant factor in shaping that opinion.

A study conducted by researchers at the University of Toledo found that people judge a person's trustworthiness, competence, and likeability based on their appearance. Similarly, in the dental sector, the appearance of the team can impact the perception of the practice. It's essential that team members maintain a consistent and professional appearance.

When team members look their best, guests and patients are more likely to perceive the business as high-quality. This is another factor that impacts the conversations patients will have about your practice. Put together your own practice style guide, allowing enough flexibility yet still guiding the team to stay 'on-brand'.

Sound the part

Many of us have two different speaking styles. The voice and language we use with our friends and family may differ greatly from the one we use in our professional life. When socialising, we often relax our language and use slang or colloquialisms that have no place in a work environment.

Being conscious of how we speak at work is essential for fostering trust with our patients that we are professionals who can deliver 5-star service. Speak slowly and clearly, and pronounce the letters in spoken words correctly, especially when conveying information about a treatment. Rapid, unclear speech can make you appear anxious or insecure. Avoid 'um's and 'ah's as this can make you sound unsure and hesitant. It is better to pause what you are saying until you have found the right words rather than littering a conversation with filler words.

Be concise! Some people habitually use the word 'like' in every sentence. 'Like, do you know what I mean, like?' Learning to speak clearly to your patients is part of building a great relationship with them. Leading hotels invest in ensuring their team members maintain a polished appearance and continuously strive to improve their communication skills.

Phone manners

The following actionable tips from the hospitality sector can be applied to the dental sector to improve phone manners:

1. **Answer the phone promptly:** A timely and courteous response can make a lasting impression on the caller. Staff should answer the phone within three rings and use a standard greeting that includes the practice name and the staff member's name. Avoid using the phrase 'How may I help?' which can send a negative signal. Many leading hotels train their staff to say, 'How may I assist you?'

2. **Be enthusiastic and attentive:** Speak in a pleasant tone and actively listen to the caller's concerns. If the caller is unclear, ask them to repeat or clarify their request to avoid confusion.

3. **Be knowledgeable and informative:** Provide the caller with the necessary information to answer their query, and if necessary, transfer them to the relevant staff member. If the staff member is not available, offer to take a message and ensure that the message is delivered promptly.

4. **Use proper phone etiquette:** Avoid interrupting the caller, typing, shuffling papers during the conversation, or eating while on the phone. Speak clearly and at an appropriate volume.

5. **End the call on a positive note:** Thank the caller for their call and personalise the end note as much as possible.

Taking messages

Taking a phone message may seem like a simple task, but it's crucial to handle it correctly to avoid misunderstandings and missed opportunities. Here are some tips on how to take a phone message:

1. **Be attentive**: Listen carefully to the caller and repeat the message to confirm that you have understood it correctly.
2. **Record all relevant information**: Take note of the caller's name, phone number, message content, and any other essential details related to the call.
3. **Use the phonetic alphabet**: In case you need clarification on any words or spellings, use the phonetic alphabet to ensure accurate transcription of the message.
4. **Implement an SOP for message handling**: Use a message template and follow a standard operating procedure (SOP) to ensure consistency and accuracy in message handling. Communicate all messages within 10 minutes of receiving the call to ensure prompt follow-up. **See page 194 on Standard operating procedures**.
5. **Provide context**: If the message requires follow-up or further action, provide context to the person who will receive the message. Include any relevant background information or previous communication related to the message. In conclusion, taking a phone message requires attentiveness, accuracy, and clear communication. By following these tips and implementing an SOP for message handling, businesses can ensure that all messages are recorded accurately and acted upon promptly. Clear communication and attention to detail are critical to ensuring customer satisfaction and building a strong relationship with clients.

   It's a huge fail if a patient calls your practice starting with 'I was told someone would call me back' and it turns out the message was not passed on, or the contact details were taken down incorrectly.

Interdepartmental communications

Positive interdepartmental relations are important to the success of any dental practice. Effective communication between team members facilitates collaboration, enhances productivity, and supports decision-making. Research has shown that businesses with strong interdepartmental communication and collaboration have higher levels of employee engagement and job satisfaction.

Studies have also shown that better communication and collaboration between team members leads to improved patient outcomes and satisfaction rates. Effective communication can also facilitate better resource allocation, resulting in more cost-effective and streamlined operations.

To promote positive interdepartmental relations, it is advisable to invest in team-building activities. Training that enhances communication skills among team members is also recommended. This ensures that everyone understands their roles and responsibilities, fosters positive relationships, and promotes engagement and productivity.

At Digimax, I say that if a team member hasn't acknowledged your email, then assume they haven't received it. This has saved many potential embarrassing situations. Establish protocols and procedures within your practice to prevent miscommunications from occurring.

The price of incomplete appreciation

There was a steak restaurant I frequented often. It was perfect for hitting my diet macros, and the food was always cooked to perfection. Plus, the service was speedy and the atmosphere inviting. I loved going there.

One day, as I walked in, the manager saw me and greeted me with a smile. When the bill came, I noticed a discount. Curious, I asked him why he gave me a discount. He replied, 'I noticed you're a regular, and I wanted to show my appreciation. From now on, every time you visit, you'll receive a 10% discount.'

I was taken aback by the manager's generosity and expressed my gratitude. Although I'm not someone who expects or seeks discounts, I still felt great knowing that I was appreciated as a customer.

But the next time I visited, the manager wasn't there, and there was no discount on the bill. The same thing happened the following time. I found myself naturally wondering each time I entered the restaurant if the manager would be there.

While I appreciated the manager's attempt to show his appreciation for my patronage, the incomplete details and lack of formal offer left me confused and uncertain. In a way, I ended up paying more than I needed to each time I visited.

This experience taught me an important lesson about offering unique benefits to customers: think through every scenario. A half-thought-out attempt to be generous or thoughtful can backfire and cause confusion, leading to brand disconnect. So, if you're going to offer a unique benefit or discount, make sure the details are clear, formal, and well-communicated to avoid misunderstandings.

TODA
SPECI
Fres
FuLL
Fis

Consistency is key

Consistency is essential to building trust and loyalty with patients. If patients receive a different experience each time they visit a practice, it can be confusing and frustrating for them. This inconsistency can make it difficult for patients to establish a strong connection with the practice, leading them to seek care elsewhere.

When patients consistently receive high-quality service during every interaction, it cultivates trust and familiarity. Consistency establishes clear expectations and guidelines for the team, resulting in heightened productivity and motivation. Consider the regular establishments you frequent; isn't it comforting to know that each visit promises an identical experience? As creatures of habit, humans thrive on consistency.

However, if the service levels are inconsistent, customers may perceive this as a decline in service quality. This can erode trust and damage the practice's reputation, leading to decreased patient loyalty and negative word of mouth.

To ensure consistency in customer service, it is important to establish clear guidelines and standard operating procedures for every member of staff. This should be outlined in a customer service manual that specifies how each team member should treat patients at every touchpoint. By working towards the same consistently high levels of customer service, the practice can ensure that every patient receives an exceptional experience every time they visit.

Establishing clear guidelines and expectations and ensuring that every team member adheres to them will lead to increased patient satisfaction, retention, and positive word of mouth.

Email ethos

Despite over 347 billion emails sent daily in 2022, many businesses lack proper email etiquette. Email training is often overlooked in training processes.

To achieve 5-star customer service standards, emails should have a consistent feel. Quality control standards should be in place to maintain a similar style across all emails, regardless of the sender, which ensures an organised and reliable appearance that is consistent with the practice's brand. Emails can be legally binding, and errors in spelling and grammar are not acceptable.

Embracing 5-star email etiquette can help prevent digital disasters and establish strong patient relationships. This can be achieved by following a few key principles. Firstly, always greet the recipient by name, and use a proper salutation such as 'Dear' or 'Good Morning / Afternoon / Evening.' Using a person's name and a friendly personalised greeting creates a connection with the recipient and shows that you value their time and communication.

It's important to use a clear and concise subject line that accurately summarises the content of the email. Change the subject line on replies, if the topic has changed significantly. This helps the recipient prioritise and categorise the email for future reference. Keep the email itself brief and to the point, focusing on the key message or request. We live in an age of low attention spans!

Emails are a representation of the business, and errors can make the business appear unprofessional and careless. Use correct spelling, grammar, punctuation, and sentence structure to ensure that the email is easy to read and understand.

Embracing 5-star email etiquette is crucial for businesses, including dental practices, to maintain professionalism, establish strong patient relationships, and avoid digital disasters. Proper email etiquette is not only about following a set of rules but also about respecting the recipient's time and communication. Consistency is key in maintaining strong patient relationships and preventing errors in email communication.

One team member shouldn't say 'Hi,' another 'hello,' another 'dear,' and another 'To.' This is not a 5-star customer service standard.

Email etiquette

1. Use a clear and concise subject line that summarises the purpose of the email. Avoid vague or misleading subject lines.

2. Use a greeting that is appropriate for the recipient and the context of the email. For example, 'Hi [Name]' is appropriate for a colleague, while 'Dear / Good Morning / Afternoon / Evening [Name]' is better suited for a patient.

3. Keep font styles and sizes consistent, refer to your brand guidelines.

4. If you have included any attachments, make sure to mention them.

5. Use an active proof-reading tool, such as Grammarly, always!

6. Re-read your email with a focus on spotting errors.

7. Write your email before entering any email addresses to avoid accidentally sending anything before it's ready.

8. Double-check you have the correct recipient and the correct email address.

9. Double-check if you're replying or replying to all.

10. Be careful not to send a patient an internal email that is not intended for them. This mistake does occur sometimes when the discussion is about the patient.

11. Use a professional email signature that includes your name, job title, and contact information.

12. Avoid using slang, jargon, or overly casual language.

13. Use paragraphs and formatting to break up large blocks of text and make your email easier to read.

14. Use active voice and clear, direct language to communicate your message effectively.

15. Be mindful of cultural differences.

16. Avoid using excessive exclamation points, as they can come across as unprofessional or insincere.

17. Keep emails to the point! Most people have a low attention span, and often will miss important aspects of your email if there is too much content.

18. Get to the point as early in the email as you can. Ideally within the first few lines of the email.

Happy staff, happy patients

Moodiness and toxicity at work can show and is contagious, it can trickle over into the service you provide. Conversely, it's easy to tell when people are happy and enjoy their job; they smile more, they're friendlier and eager to help.

One study that demonstrates the negative impact of a toxic team member on the overall team's performance is a 2015 study published in the *Journal of Applied Psychology*. The study found that employees who had experienced negative behaviour from a colleague were more likely to engage in counterproductive work behaviours themselves, leading to decreased team cohesion and lower overall team performance.

The study surveyed 111 teams from various industries and found that teams with a toxic member experienced lower levels of trust, communication, and cooperation among team members. These negative effects were particularly pronounced when the toxic member had high negative affectivity, which refers to the tendency to experience negative emotions and express negative attitudes.

The study also found that teams with a toxic member were more likely to experience turnover, as employees who were exposed to negative behaviour were more likely to leave the organisation. Overall, the study highlights the importance of addressing toxic behaviour in the workplace, as it can have far-reaching negative consequences for the team and the organisation as a whole. Efforts must be taken to acknowledge exceptional performance by the team and actively prevent the spread of toxicity within the organisation.

Efforts must be taken to acknowledge exceptional performance by the team and actively prevent the spread of toxicity within the practice. Toxic behaviour can spread like a virus and poison the workplace culture, ultimately causing serious damage to your team and brand. **See page 207 on Employee recognition and page 211 on Personal Development.**

DiSC profiles

Building a great team is as much about personalities as it is skills and qualifications. The DiSC profile is a personal assessment tool practice managers can use to measure personality and behaviour styles to improve productivity, teamwork, and communication.

The DiSC profile consists of four key profile points.

Dominance: How direct and strong-willed someone is
Influence: How sociable, talkative, and lively someone is
Steadiness: How gentle, accommodating, and soft-hearted someone is
Conscientiousness: How analytical and logical someone is

We all have an element of each profile within our personalities, but most people tend to fall into one or two of the four main DiSC profiles. Assessing your employees with this tool can help you build the perfect team. For instance, if every employee falls under the dominance profile, chances are there'll be many strong-willed characters butting heads. Ensuring a mix of personality types can create balance and harmony, leading to excellent customer service.

Understanding the DiSC profile can provide several benefits in the workplace. For example, it can help team members and managers to communicate more effectively, build stronger relationships, and work more collaboratively. By identifying their own and others' personality traits and communication styles, team members can adjust their communication and behaviour to better connect with others and work towards common goals.

Additionally, the DiSC profile can also help identify potential conflicts or misunderstandings that may arise due to personality differences. By recognising and addressing these conflicts early on, teams can prevent them from escalating and disrupting productivity.

Recruiting service superstars

When it comes to building a great service team, hiring for attitude, enthusiasm, and positivity is just as important as hiring for skills and experience. In fact, studies have shown that these qualities can be even more important than technical ability in determining an employee's success in a customer-facing role.

So, how do you identify and attract service superstars during the recruitment process?

First and foremost, it's important to focus on attitude. Look for candidates who have a positive outlook, a strong work ethic, and a willingness to learn and grow. Ask questions that probe for their approach to customer service and how they handle challenging situations. Be on the lookout for candidates who are empathetic, resourceful, and proactive.

Enthusiasm is another key factor to consider. Look for candidates who are genuinely excited about the prospect of working with customers and who show enthusiasm for the job and the company. Candidates who have a natural ability to engage with people and who can bring energy and enthusiasm to their interactions are likely to excel in a customer-facing role. Positivity is also crucial. Candidates who have a positive outlook, who are solution-focused, and who can maintain a sense of optimism even in the face of challenges are likely to be effective in a customer-facing role. Ask questions that assess their ability to stay positive and focused when dealing with difficult situations.

It's important to create a recruitment process that reflects your company's commitment to service excellence. From the language used in job postings to the questions asked during interviews, make sure your recruitment process reflects your company's values and priorities. Hiring for attitude, enthusiasm, and positivity is essential when building a service team. Look for candidates who exhibit these qualities, create a recruitment process that reflects your values, and watch as your team of service superstars excels in delighting your customers.

You just can't get the staff

You just can't get the staff. It's a phrase heard all too often in the business world, as leaders struggle to find the right team members to meet their high standards. But this limiting belief needs to be challenged. It's not that the skilled professionals don't exist; it's that the recruitment process and training culture may be flawed. I agree that the talent pool may appear to be shrinking, but we still witness businesses operating at exceptional standards. The question is, why are they able to attract and retain staff while you struggle? Are you advertising only when you have a vacancy to fill? It is advisable to advertise consistently throughout the year, so you can build a talent bank to tap into when a vacancy arises.

We expect team members to act like business owners but often we haven't given them the tools to do so. With the right attitude and willingness to learn, anyone can be a valuable self-thinking team member. Don't let this limiting mindset hold you back from discovering new opportunities when building a team.

Yes, recruiting top talent may seem harder than ever before, but successful businesses still manage to do it, and do it well. If you're struggling to find the right applicants, expand your search and take a hard look at your company's online presence. Does it look like a place people would want to work?

And when you do find the right staff, make sure you're investing in their training and providing regular appraisals. If things still aren't working out, review your company culture and leadership approach. Don't let the 'can't get the staff' mentality become an excuse for not achieving success.

Hiring like a boss

Proactive recruitment

- Jobs advertised throughout the year, even if no current vacancies.
- Informal telephone conversations held with standout candidates, emphasising a willingness to learn.
- Thoughtful questions used to evaluate emotional intelligence.
- Shortlisting candidates through basic comprehension tests (remote test and dependent on role).
- Passing candidates invited for a compelling pitch session by you, highlighting why your practice is an incredible place to work at.
- Candidates showing interest proceed to one-on-one interviews, providing an opportunity to discuss skills in-depth.
- Team members can take the candidate to lunch, addressing any queries.
- A collaborative decision made with the candidate to determine if a mutually beneficial partnership exists, leading to a formal offer.
- Due to a smaller candidate pool we may face post-Brexit, you can develop a website landing page featuring a video from your principal and team members, passionately conveying why your practice is the ultimate workplace.
- Recognise the changing landscape of employment and the importance of meeting candidates' genuine desires beyond financial considerations.
- Seek individuals who share your vision and are dedicated to providing the best possible service to your patients, no matter the challenge.

Taking a unique approach will allow you to stand out from the crowd and appeal to the most ambitious, enthusiastic, and best fits for the roles.

Quality staff training

Training = Learning.

We all learn differently. Some people are able to pick up new skills from reading textbooks, while others need a more hands-on, visual, or auditory approach. And when it comes to the hotel industry, you'll find a wide range of team members – from undiscovered geniuses to those who need a bit of extra practice to really shine.

But here's the thing: no matter where your team members fall on the spectrum, providing regular training is key to developing quality staff. Even if it means repeating or reviewing the same information. It's important to avoid comparing team members and to recognise that everyone's abilities vary. If you've hired people who are enthusiastic, willing to learn, and have a positive attitude, it's up to you to invest in their growth and development.

Team members who feel confident in their abilities are happier and more productive on the job, and that's good news for everyone. The best hotels in the world recognise that training is not a one-time event, but an ongoing process. This is especially true for customer service training, which is critical for providing a memorable and enjoyable guest experience.

When you take the time to teach your employees, you show them that you value their contribution and are invested in their success. By growing their knowledge base and improving their skills, you'll make them more effective in the workplace and help them become more confident team members. And when your team feels like productive members of your organisation, it not only encourages them to perform better, but it also improves morale across the board.

Hospitality standard customer service training is a great way to ensure that your team understands what you expect of them. Whether it's through this book or the 5-star hospitality customer service visiting workshop available on **clinics.co.uk**, you'll provide them with the tools and resources they need to succeed. By creating a customer service manual and adhering to it, you'll establish clear standards and expectations for your team. And by using it to train new recruits, you'll ensure that everyone is on the same page.

In the end, investing in staff training is an investment in the success of your business. With the proper investment in training, you'll find that most team members will flourish and grow into valuable members of your organisation.

At Digimax, we offer 'Digimax University,' a continuously evolving training program designed to adapt to the ever-changing landscape.

Customer service manual

A customer service training manual in the hospitality industry is at the heart of staff training but also sets out staff operating standards. Operating standards form part of the employee guidelines and how they must always conduct themselves. This comprehensive guide should contain all the essential information your team will need to provide exceptional personalised customer service.

It should include all the basics, such as how to answer the phone and greet patients in person, answer questions and deal with enquiries, and deal with and address any patient complaints. The manual should cover almost every aspect of customer service a business should have.

The more bullet-pointed information your manual includes, the easier it will be for employees to deliver a consistently high level of service across the board. This is because they will all be reading from the same page, and as I mentioned on **page 173**, consistency is critical to delivering excellent customer service. I found it incredible for new staff hires, as they learn from day one that you are an exceptional business, and the standards are high!

You should be mindful, however, that your customer service manual is only a guide. It cannot teach essential personal skills that every staff member should have, such as kindness, common sense, or politeness. Still, it will help all team members navigate everyday situations professionally and efficiently.

In 5-star hotels, managers often refer to customer service training materials to remind the team of service expectations. It also allows you to refer back to expectations that are written in black and white, so there is no or minimal areas of doubt for a team member.

Make sure to update your manual regularly and ask for team input. Your team will better understand the day-to-day nuances within your practice. In addition, it should be encouraged to provide valuable recommendations on improving recurring challenges through upgrading your customer service systems. Asking the team for input shows that you value their knowledge and experience, which works towards building a great collaborative team.

In the hotel industry, the stakes are high – a single poor experience for a guest can lead to severe damage and the loss of repeat business. That's why I take service very seriously in my business at Digimax. I believe that it's essential for any business to be a bit 'over the top' when it comes to service.

Providing exceptional service is not for the faint of heart – it requires a tireless commitment to detail and a relentless pursuit of excellence. By investing in staff training and holding your team members to high standards, you can create a culture of excellence that sets your practice apart from the rest, just like the best hotels in the world.

Ultimately, the success of a 5-star hotel or practice depends on the guest experience. By prioritising service and consistently delivering on your promises, you can build a loyal base of repeat patients who trust and appreciate your commitment to quality. So don't be afraid to be over the top – your patients will thank you and rave about you.

At our 5-star customer service training workshop, we provide a manual that you can easily adapt to your own practice. Visit **clinics.co.uk** to learn more.

Understanding generation mute

As a member of the 'generation mute,' I understand the frustration that can come with businesses trying to force communication in a way that is not preferred. Just because I send an email doesn't mean I want to receive a phone call in response. And it's not just me. A survey by Ofcom found that only 15% of 16- to 24-year-olds believed phone calls were the most important method of communication.

So, if a patient chooses to communicate with your practice through a certain medium, don't change it without good reason or permission. If a patient is WhatsApping your business, there's a reason they chose that method, and it's essential to respect that choice.

I've experienced situations where a business kept calling me repeatedly, even after I had asked a simple question over email. It's frustrating and shows a lack of understanding of how I prefer to communicate. Patients want to communicate in the medium they propose, and it's vital to meet them where they are.

Of course, there may be reasons to change the communication medium. For example, taking a patient off of WhatsApp and redirecting them to a website URL to book a physical consultation. But these decisions should be made with consideration and permission.

It's easy to criticise new modes of behaviour, but the reality is that communication preferences change, and practices need to adapt to keep up. As 24-year-old Eleanor Halls wrote in *The Times*, an unexpected phone call can cause anxiety. So, it's crucial to shape your practice around your patients' communication preferences and understand that what works for one patient may not work for another.

Standard operating procedures

Standard Operating Procedures (SOPs) are a 'how to' step-by-step guide on completing tasks correctly and efficiently. They are designed to be executable by any capable person. Therefore, no 'reading between the lines' should be required... if your standard operating procedure is bulletproof.

I know the CEO of a leading chain of Italian restaurants in London. He showed me their SOP on how to cook an egg whilst, in the same sentence, he told me he employs chefs who once worked in famous kitchens worldwide. I asked, 'You teach leading chefs how to cook an egg?'. He looked at me and said 'Shaz, if you ate eggs at my restaurant in Regent Street, and then the next day went for the same eggs, but in my Knightsbridge restaurant and the texture, size, shape, and taste differed... how would that make you feel?' The question was also the answer to my question.

5-star hotels use SOPs to ensure all staff follows the same procedures to deliver high-quality customer service, such as how to greet guests, the check-in process, housekeeping policy, room service checklists, and so on, so key guest touchpoints are executed in the same consistent way every time! You should also create SOPs for day-to-day customer service activities within your practice.

Using an SOP is a way to ensure consistency with all staff working to the same guidelines of high-quality service. They can also improve efficiency, minimise mistakes, and provide patients with a smooth and hassle-free customer experience. SOPs mean that everyone performs to your brand's deliverability expectations, and there is no reliance on a specific team member. I know businesses that collapse in their delivery when a service star is off work for a few days. Great companies don't make this mistake.

Take the time to make your SOPs clear and concise so that it is easy to follow for all. Make sure to include the purpose of the SOP, any limitations, and its intended usage. Outline each necessary step and use imagery or elementary diagrams if required. Making it easy for staff to follow standard operating procedures allows you to deliver 5-star customer service consistently and efficiently.

Multiple reps build muscle

Small changes can make a big impact. Anyone who has ever tried to get fit and healthy knows how overwhelming it can be to make significant changes overnight. The thought of suddenly having to run five miles a day can be so daunting that many people don't even make it to the starting line. The trick is to start small. Begin by walking every day, then gradually build up to a slow and gentle jog. As your fitness levels increase, you'll find that you can run for longer periods each day. A year from now, you'll look back and thank yourself for starting small.

The same principle applies to business. Big changes can require significant time, effort, and expense, making them so daunting that it's easy not to start. Instead of trying to improve one thing by 10%, consider improving ten things by just 1%.

As a business owner with over 20 years of experience, I know that even the best systems aren't perfect. That's why I take every opportunity to improve my processes and procedures, no matter how minor the adjustment may seem. When a team member brings a new idea for improvement, I commend their initiative and act on great ideas without delay.

Making minor changes is easier to achieve and maintain, leading to a greater chance of success. When we achieve our goals, it motivates us to keep going, which in turn, leads to much bigger changes overall. So, don't be afraid to start small and celebrate each milestone along the way.

Be SMART

Establishing goals and objectives within a practice is an effective approach to ensure successful outcomes. Utilising the SMART formula makes it simpler to identify, track progress, and accomplish those goals.

S – Specific

Set specific goals about what you want your team to achieve. If the goal is ambiguous, you'll never truly know if they've achieved it or not!

M – Measurable

Being able to measure the goals will help you to know where they are succeeding and where they can improve.

A – Attainable

Don't set yourself or your team up for failure with unattainable goals! Make sure that any objectives you set are realistically achievable.

R – Relevant

Are the goals relevant to your business or team development? Will achieving them impact positively for the individual, the team, or your patients?

T – Time

Set a timeframe in which to achieve the goals. If there's no set time limit, there's no pressure. Having an 'end' to the goal allows you to know if you or your employee have achieved it.

Here is a non-SMART goal:

Vague:	Increase patient retention rates.

Here is a SMART goal:

Specific:	Increase patient retention rates by 10% in the next six months.
Measurable:	Use our practice management software to track patient retention rates on a monthly basis and report progress to the team.
Achievable:	Implement a patient loyalty program that rewards patients for referrals and consistent attendance at appointments.
Relevant:	Improving patient retention rates will result in increased revenue for the practice and improved patient outcomes.
Time-bound:	Achieve the 10% increase in patient retention rates within the next six months.

Customer service staff reviews

Employee performance reviews are already a part of your practice. Though have you considered having reviews with team members with the sole topic being about customer service standards?

Imagine the impact this will have on your practice compared to most practices that don't do this.

Schedule regular customer service reviews with your team and use some of the questions on the next page to understand where things are going well and where they can be improved.

Team customer service review questions

The below are examples, just to give you an idea of the kind of questions you could be asking:

1. Have you heard any constructive or negative comments from a patient recently? If so, could you share them with me and suggest ways we could address them?
2. What are your thoughts on how we could enhance our customer service? Are there any areas where we could improve our approach or practices?
3. Have you implemented any improvements based on the feedback received from our patients? If so, could you share your experience and the outcomes achieved?
4. How can we encourage more positive Google reviews from our patients? Are there any additional steps we can take to enhance their experience?
5. Lastly, can you share any SMART goals you have in mind that could help us achieve the objectives discussed above? Let's brainstorm and discuss ways to continuously improve our customer service together.

Mystery shoppers

A great way of getting an honest, impartial opinion on your team's customer service standards is by using mystery shoppers.

Your mystery shopper will be able to give you a first-hand account of their experience, what they liked, any wow moments, and what they think could be improved.

There are companies you can engage with to conduct mystery shopping for you. These companies may offer more meticulous reporting, ensuring that all aspects are thoroughly covered.

Employee recognition

Here are 4 statistics that demonstrate the importance of recognising and valuing employees in the workplace.

1. According to a study by Achievers, 93% of employees who feel valued at work are more motivated to do their best.
2. A survey by Glassdoor found that 4 out of 5 employees would prefer recognition over a pay raise.
3. Gallup research shows that companies with high levels of employee engagement have 21% higher profitability than those with low levels of engagement, and recognition is a key factor in boosting engagement.
4. A survey by SHRM found that companies with recognition programs have a lower turnover rate than those without, with recognition being cited as one of the top drivers of employee retention.

It's an incredible feeling to be recognised and acknowledged for our efforts when we pour our heart and soul into our work and produce something we're proud of.

Recognising and rewarding your team for a job well done can have a significant impact on their morale and performance. When employees feel valued and appreciated for their hard work and contributions, it gives them a sense of ownership and accomplishment. This recognition makes them feel like an integral part of the team, encourages them to maintain high standards of work, and can even increase employee retention.

A simple 'thank you, great job' can make someone's day, but when employees go above and beyond, it's important to show appreciation.

Team days or evenings out are also fantastic ways to say 'thank you' after everyone has worked well. They provide an opportunity for employees to bond outside of the work environment and can help strengthen team dynamics.

It's worth noting that I don't believe in rewarding people for simply doing their job. Fulfilling their job duties is a two-way agreement, and doing more than what's expected is what deserves recognition.

Personal development

We should all undertake personal development in our day-to-day lives, whether for personal or professional advancement. Any time we make a conscious effort to better ourselves, we participate in personal development. It doesn't just refer to a specific time in our lives but rather an ongoing awareness of educating ourselves and a concerted effort to consistently grow and improve.

In our professional lives, it can further our careers, improve our knowledge, and help us become more productive, well-rounded workers.

Helping your team with their personal development benefits not only them but also you, your practice, and ultimately your patients. Working with your employees to develop further skills, either by way of external training or in-house, hands-on practical training can not only improve their knowledge but also help them grow their confidence.

I always try to take an interest in my team members' personal challenges, provided they're comfortable sharing. With the extra years I may have on some of them, I could offer guidance or even direct help to navigate through their struggles. It's possible that addressing these challenges could make their life easier and bring more positivity to their work. A team member with a happier life outside of work is more likely to come to work with a positive attitude and bring their A-game.

ESTABLISHING RELATIONSHIPS

Building your emotional bank account

In customer service, it's essential to build a positive relationship with patients. This relationship is built over time, much like a bank account. Every positive interaction is like a deposit, while every negative interaction is like a withdrawal. The goal is to maintain a high balance in your 'emotional bank account' by making more deposits than withdrawals.

Positive interactions can come in many forms, from a friendly greeting to a kind word or a thoughtful gesture. A simple smile or asking how a patient's day is going can go a long way in building rapport. These positive interactions make patients feel valued and appreciated, leading to a more positive experience overall.

On the other hand, negative interactions can quickly deplete your emotional bank account. Offering an indifferent or weak service can cause patients to lose trust and confidence in your practice. These negative interactions can result in patients taking their business elsewhere or leaving negative reviews, damaging your practice's reputation.

It's important to note that building your emotional bank account takes time and effort. Consistency is key, and every interaction counts. While a single positive interaction may not have a significant impact, a series of positive interactions over time can create a deep and meaningful connection with patients.

The more frequent and significant deposits you make into the emotional bank account, the less likely your account will be overdrawn by a patient complaint, especially when things don't go as planned for any reason.

Professional small talk

We all know someone that can talk for England! That bubbly, chatty, extroverted friend or family member who can always find something to talk about means you're never left with awkward silences. The more introverted of us may not find it as easy to speak so freely and effortlessly; however, mastering the art of small talk is vital for building relationships with patients.

It's not always easy to make conversation out of nothing. Still, the discomfort of making conversation is infinitely easier than the discomfort of standing in silence. Silences increase tension and awkwardness and can make the interaction uncomfortable and strained. Creating and maintaining some conversation with your patients is essential.

While small talk may come more naturally to some, there are some simple tips to keep conversations going for those that struggle, the most crucial being to listen! Often you can simply listen and respond to what your patient is saying. Perhaps they've turned up to an appointment late and mentioned that there was a lot of traffic, you can ask them where they travelled from, or if they managed to find parking easily. If they mention that they've just come from lunch, ask where they went and what they had to eat. It's easy to make small talk if you simply listen and respond.

If your patient is shy and introverted, there are some easy ways to get the conversation started. See the next page on breaking the ice.

Breaking the ice

One of the easiest ways to break the ice with a patient and initiate a conversation is to ask open-ended questions. Here are 9 examples of open-ended questions used in a hotel setting. Use these to inspire you to create your own ones:

1. How's the weather treating you today?
2. What brings you to our hotel today?
3. Have you visited our city before?
4. Is there anything you're hoping to see or do during your stay?
5. Are there any requests we can assist you with?
6. How was your journey here?
7. Do you have any questions about our hotel facilities?
8. Have you dined at any local restaurants that you would recommend?
9. Is there anything else we can do to make your stay more enjoyable?

By asking questions that require more than a simple yes or no reply, the patient must respond with more information which opens the conversation and leads to further opportunities to ask more questions. Use the tips on the next page to break the ice with your patients!

Ice breakers

Compliments
Notice something nice about the patient and give them a sincere compliment.

Family
Most people will light up at the opportunity to talk about their children.

Plans for the day or weekend
Are they doing anything fun or going anywhere nice?

Traffic and transport
How did they get here? Was it an easy journey?

Weather
If you're British, this should come naturally!

Holidays
You could ask if they have any upcoming holiday plans.

RICHMOND
THE
SMILE
STÜDIOS
Dear Patient,
It's that time again.. we
miss you and need you to
come in for your
examination.
Please call
team
book

Postcards

Whether pre-appointment or post-appointment, you can maintain great patient relationships with some fun and/or educational postcards. These can help relax your patients in advance of their appointments and provide them with any information they might not have been aware of that could benefit them in their daily lives.

Don't underestimate the power of snail mail! Sending out post-appointment cards can be as easy as a heartfelt thank-you or a few tips on after-care. Get creative and consider including brushing techniques, motivational quotes, or even a witty joke or two. It's a great opportunity to involve your entire team and brainstorm fun ideas. Not only will this activity foster a stronger bond within your practice, but your patients will feel appreciated and cared for knowing that you're thinking of them long after their appointment has ended.

Gifts

Gifts are always a nice touch, but useful gifts serve as a reminder long after the patient has left the surgery. The obvious choices are good quality personalised mirrors, lip balms, and oral hygiene kits, but don't be afraid to think outside the box or adopt a more personalised approach.

It might be that your patient has mentioned they're travelling to New York for the first time. Be one step ahead by surprising them with a city guide! The fact that you've taken the time to listen to them and find something they will use or appreciate is a whole new level of customer service 'wow'!

HOW TO
BE AN
EXPLORER
OF THE
WORLD

Be proactive

Proactive businesses will always win in the reputation game than over the reactive ones. Reactive customer service waits until there is an issue to 'react' to, while proactive customer service works hard to ensure those issues don't arise in the first place!

Being proactive allows you to anticipate patient needs and prepare for any unexpected developments, rather than finding yourself on the back foot and dealing with a patient reactively. Usually, a sequence of failures leads to a complaint when the patient has had enough. What was a minor initial miscommunication, turns into a huge deal because other problems appeared down the line in the customer service journey.

Take your health as an example. Someone proactive will exercise, eat healthily, and take general care of their body. A reactive person will wait until they feel ill or have to go to a doctor before addressing their overall health. It is harder to get well than it is to stay well.

Being proactive also gives you greater control over your brand. It allows you to create your own situations and narrative in which you can succeed and deliver high-quality services and treatments to your patients. You shouldn't be waiting for things to go wrong or for patients to complain before fixing things – being one step ahead and proactively looking at how you can improve your customer service will save you reactive headaches down the road.

At Digimax, we send a physical gift via post to new enquiries. However, we realised that some of our enquirers are associates who are in the early stages of considering opening their own practice. We thought about the possibility of sending the gift to their work address but realised this could create an awkward situation for the associate if their team members aren't aware of their plans. To avoid this, we ask, 'Can we use this address as your mailing address?' This small detail could prevent a bigger problem, as we always like to take a proactive approach.

The pro-active car lease company that goes quiet...

I was busy and kept missing calls and emails from a car leasing company eager to renew my lease. Despite finding their persistence a bit annoying, it was clear they were keen to secure my business.

When I am in need of a service, a pro-active approach will always win for me over a company that is low on steam, lukewarm in their follow up and support. So, with the full awareness of knowing how poor many companies are at keeping in touch, I treated their approach as a 'plus' for them and placed my order.

After I placed my order – radio silence. No updates on delivery dates. It was always me chasing, and the answers were becoming vaguer, and the delivery date was pushed further into the future. Once, I called up for an update (I hate calling!), and I was promised a callback with more information. Again, no news, so I called up the very next day and reminded him that he had promised to return my call, to which he said, 'Ah, sorry, the manufacturer didn't get back to me.'

At that point, I had to give him a 101 in customer service for free (if this book was printed, I would be throwing it at him with great force). He did reply telling me they are overwhelmed, short-staffed. That isn't good enough, if you want sympathy then at least send an email to all your clients that you are going to be a cr*p company for a bit. Even that would be nicer than me having to chase for updates.

The point I am making here, the company will never get a referral from me. All the hard work of their sales team in making strong first impressions is completely down the drain. In a dental practice environment, this could be the hard work of the dentist spending time with the patient, really going through a comprehensive assessment and then reception not keeping promises, making mistakes and just creating an inconvenience for the patient. It happens far too frequently.

Become part of your patients' story

We are all protagonists in the stories in our heads! Our daily routines – brewing coffee before work, catching the train, grabbing breakfast at the local café – are all part of our individual stories. When you become part of your patient's story and deliver unexpected moments of joy or wonder to punctuate the everyday grind, you can make memories and interrupt the narrative.

People buy feelings and experiences, not just products or services. When faced with multiple choices, we will often choose a brand that we feel aligned with, so having a good understanding of your brand ethos is key to understanding how to align yourself with your patients.

When you make someone feel good or valued, treat them with respect, and deliver exceptional wow service, you become part of their story. When it's a unique story, patients are likely to tell others.

Make your patients the hero

When marketing their goods or services, many businesses make themselves the hero – 'My treatment can do this' or 'Our practice offers that.'

While this is vital information to help promote your brand, when you make your patients the hero, you create a connection with your audience and prospective patients that they are the most important aspect of your business.

Burger King's slogan isn't 'We're the best burger in the world'; it's 'Have it your way'. Their slogan puts their customers at the heart of their messaging and connects with them more emotionally.

When you focus on what your patients will receive rather than what you are providing, you make them the hero of your story and theirs.

Social media has changed the landscape for heroes. When patients are overjoyed with their smile transformation, they'll want to share it with the world. With their permission, you can also share the results with your followers, showing prospective patients just how transformational your treatments are.

Sainsbury's and the tiger bread

It's not often that supermarkets change their products on the advice of customers, let alone 3-year-old ones, but that's precisely what the UK supermarket, Sainsbury's, did for a young girl called Lily Robinson.

Lily was confused by the naming of Sainsbury's 'tiger bread' because the shape and style of the crust looked much more like a giraffe! With help from her parents, Lily wrote to Sainsbury's to tell them as such. To their surprise, they received a reply from Sainsbury's customer service manager, wholeheartedly agreeing with them!

Within the reply was the line, 'I think renaming tiger bread giraffe bread is a brilliant idea.'

Lily's mother enjoyed the reply so much that she shared it on her blog, where it went viral. The feedback from the internet was resounding – the bread definitely looked more like a giraffe than a tiger. And Sainsbury's listened! The bread was renamed to giraffe bread, and the supermarket even put little notes about the name change next to the bread display, as a nod to Lily and her original 'complaint.'

Sainsbury's took the time to reply, genuinely and thoughtfully. Then, they listened to Lily, then to the online feedback. Finally, they acted on the feedback. Every step of the way, Sainsbury's provided first-rate customer service, and in doing so, made a young girl and the rest of the internet very happy!

Build patient loyalty

Human beings are creatures of habit. When we find something we like, we tend to stick with it. The same goes for businesses; when you

- Provide treatment that meets patients' expectations
- Personalise your service through customer service
- Make patients feel special through culture, detail, and attention
- Deliver a consistent experience every time

You increase the likelihood of patients becoming repeat customers and vocal advocates for your brand.

Consistent delivery is a crucial component of brand loyalty. Patients return because they know what to expect. Take Nando's as an example: I know exactly what I'll receive when I go there. I can't recall an instance where the food, welcome, presentation, communication, waiting times, comfort, or interior varied enough to confuse me. This consistency has made me a loyal customer. The same principle applies to most businesses I patronise. Delivering a consistent experience every time is crucial.

Poor communication is often the root cause of problems. A patient may not complain, but they might not be impressed enough to rave about your practice. Therefore, it's essential to ensure the entire team is focused on creating a positive patient experience that turns every ideal patient into a raving fan.

Although you should strive for excellence, it's important to recognise that some patients cannot be pleased. This is true for many businesses, including leading hotels and restaurants. While you should go to great lengths to please those patients, it's equally important not to let disheartening experiences affect your delivery to other patients who do value you.

Keeping patients connected to your brand is also essential. During the pandemic, the brands I was most loyal to weren't keeping in touch with me. As a result, I started forming new habits and building relationships with brands that spoke to me. Invest in local brand awareness to stay in your patients' minds, even when they don't need you.

Peach Springs
San Luis

Develop trust from afar

Building trust with patients doesn't always start when they walk through your practice door. Research shows that customers are often 60% of the way through their buying journey before contacting a company.

I call it 'Rapport on Steroids' when a patient feels like they know you even before they sit in your chair. From your online presence, including your social media and website, to Google reviews and press endorsements, as well as word-of-mouth recommendations, all help patients build trust in you before booking a consultation or treatment. Patients who feel connected to you tend to be happier overall and more accepting when things don't always go according to plan.

Curating your brand in a way that potential patients can feel like they know you from afar instils a level of comfort and trust that they have a clear idea of who you are, what you stand for, and what level of treatment to expect. This is precisely why social media has been so successful for businesses. The rigid corporate barrier has been broken down, and we can now see the faces behind the businesses.

In my book, *Instagram for Dentists*, I delve into this topic in greater detail. Understanding your target audience and building your brand and online persona to align with their expectations is key to building their trust from afar.

Social media

By now, you should understand that exceptional customer service is based on effective communication. Social media is a powerful communication tool that allows you to showcase your personal and practice brand to the public.

Contrary to popular belief, you don't need to post choreographed dances, meals, or selfies all day to succeed on social media. In fact, the most successful dental practices that attract swarms of ideal patients aren't doing that.

Instead, use social media as another channel to showcase your practice, making patients feel like they know you before they even get in touch with you. At Digimax, we receive enquiries from individuals who were asked to call us by others. Interestingly, when we search for their names on our database, we often find that they haven't used our services before. This highlights the power of reputation and how people will recommend you to others based on it.

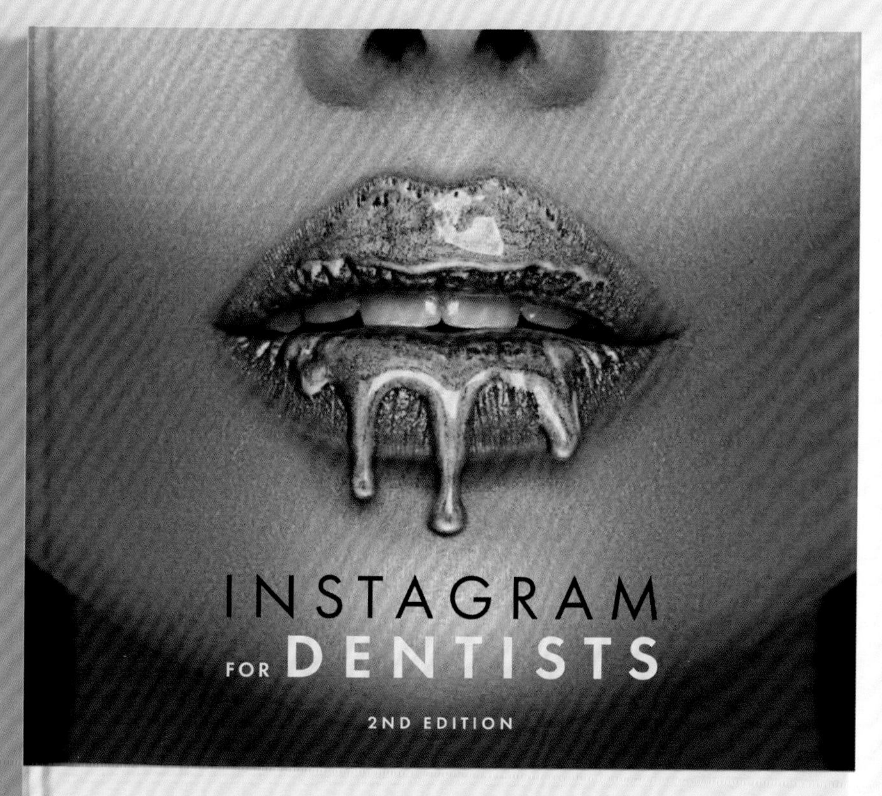
INSTAGRAM
FOR DENTISTS
2ND EDITION
BY SHAZ MEMON

Build trust with Google reviews

Most businesses now rely on online patient reviews to raise a profile and entice further custom. Indeed, patients consider Google reviews a valuable and measurable source of information. They illustrate the highs and lows of any customer/patient experience.

Many dental practices with exceptional Google ratings will stand out from their competition. Those with consistently great feedback report a boost in footfall because most new patients are relying on the views of others for reassurance in their confidence in a practice's abilities to deliver exceptional care.

But if your bank of patient testimonials is running dry or may even be non-existent, how best to boost that all-essential star rating?

Gaining Google reviews

Whilst direct requests for Google reviews may irk some as a seemingly unethical practice, it is in fact widely considered an essential tool in your marketing armoury.

Online reviews are the bedrock of any business looking to promote to a public who widely accept and utilise Google's rating system. The essence of good ethics is in avoidance of specifically requesting only positive feedback.

When you do approach patients, let your patients know you are asking for a 'favour' and explain that the practice relies on patients like them to encourage others to enjoy your services. You will quickly know whether you're asking properly based on the number of patients who respond to your review request. Be patient. You'll get better with time. Everyone does!

So, who are your patients with the best review potential? As experienced professionals, you and your staff have the benefit of hands-on experience in reading body language. This means understanding who might be open to helping you out and who might shun the idea.

Being able to ascertain whether or not someone is likely to respond enthusiastically is a start. Trust too has its part to play and, as a key factor in the clinician-patient dynamic, it is an easy option to ask someone you know well. Especially if it eradicates any awkwardness in calling on a favour.

But don't let comfortable familiarity limit you to seeking testimonials solely from long-term attendees.

The most positive feedback inevitably comes from those who have just experienced optimal care and for whom you've achieved amazing results. Ideally requesting feedback at the peak of patient satisfaction.

Making it easy

Personalise the request and mirror the language used. Observing professionalism is important. But everyone differs in the way in which they communicate in written form. Therefore, factor this skill into team training and incentivise the team.

It's key that patients have a Google account. If they don't, asking them to sign up for an account may seem too much investment. An alternative could be to ask that they leave a Facebook review instead.

For those who do have a Google account, the key is showing a patient that they must sign into Google and navigate to your business listing on Google to leave the review. Sometimes that's difficult for people to do, so make it easy for them.

Google has made it easy for businesses to direct their customers to a personalised Google review link.

Make time to walk patients through the process:

- Sign into Google (Gmail account)
- Search for your business on Google
- Click to leave a review
- Select star rating, write review, and submit

Remember that it is good etiquette to reply to Google reviews. When logged in as an owner of a business, you will see a reply button below each review. I would also send an email thanking them. Perhaps consider emailing them a referral voucher, asking for them to share with friends and family. Choosing the right time will dramatically increase the chances of them sharing it.

Directly asking each and every patient for a review of their experience may not always be feasible. So, adding a review link in all your email signatures can be helpful too.

'Ask the right few'

Jas Gill is practice principal at Moonlight Dental Surgery believes that the essence of successfully collecting Google reviews lies in teamwork.

He explains: 'Our success to date has come from working as a team to create truly achievable systems that work for everyone. Through having team meetings with all involved, and gaining team insights, we have been able to strategise and create protocols and procedures that all agree can be facilitated within a busy day.'

This has resulted in an increase in reviews. It has a side benefit of giving the team satisfaction that they are heard, that their workload is recognised and respected, and that they have contributed.

By having clear and written SMART goals, we set aside time in the week to plan and also discover where any key problem might lie. For example, we put a marker next to every patient booked in that day who has a Gmail account, and those are asked for feedback first. Trust me, it's easier to ask a few patients in a busy practice rather than telling the team to ask everyone – so why not ask the right few?

He adds: 'We also get a better response rate when we WhatsApp the patient the Google link rather than email it to them. Sometimes, we ask them for a testimonial, and then WhatsApp it to them followed by a Google link in two separate messages as it's easy to copy and paste. They can then copy the message, click on the link and paste it as a Google review leaving a star rating at the same time. These are just simple ways of removing obstacles.'

If you don't ask, you don't get.

By keeping it simple, practice owners can save time. As Jas says: 'They need to focus their ideas and avoid attempting to implement too many ideas at the same time – otherwise nothing works.'

Alternatively, some practices incentivise front-of-house staff with £5 per review. Both practices I know that do this now have more than 100 reviews. The power is in asking and telling them just how much it would mean, as one day you may be looking to enter an award.

Clinical director, Dr Carol Somerville Roberts, urges all practice teams to embark on a mission to increase the number of Google reviews with simple requests.

She says: 'You can always ask. We ask for reviews and, if the patient says 'yes', we then ask if they would like us to send them a text message with the link. We send it straight away and this has increased the number of reviews we get because it makes it easy for patients to leave one.'

It's quite simple – if you don't ask, you don't get.

Six tips for Google reviews

1. **Who?** Invite regular long-term patients well known to you by all means but do ensure a mix of demographics. Patients who are complimentary are obvious candidates.

2. **When?** I suggest immediately after treatment when they feel euphoric about the result – and, thereafter, a maximum of twice more. Do respect boundaries. Any more than three times and you run the risk of annoying your patients. When emailing a follow-up, state that leaving a review will take 30 seconds and give them an example of questions most people answer on their reviews to take away the element of having to think.

   How? Make it as easy as possible for them to feedback. Provide a personalised link to your Google review page. Positive engagement is everything – and if the feedback isn't so great, then at least you can handle any complaints swiftly and positively. When you ask, be clear that if they had any constructive feedback, alternatively they may wish to share it directly with you instead.

   To obtain your Google review link:

   a) Log in to your Google Business Profile.

   b) Google search for your business name.

   c) Look for the 'Ask for reviews' link.

   d) Click on it, and a short URL will appear.

   e) Share this URL with your patients to request reviews.

3. **Where?** A note of caution, patients can certainly leave reviews when at the practice, so long as they are not connected to your WiFi. Google has been known to remove reviews if too many are left from the same network IP address. So do make sure the patients leave their reviews either at your practice (but not whilst connected to your WiFi), or once back at home and on their own laptop/mobile/tablet using their own connection.
4. **What?** Never directly ask for a 5-star review. Select satisfied patients who you know enjoyed their experience with you. Whilst you can micro manage all of your Google reviews, you can up the odds in your favour by engaging with those who know you best.
5. **Why?** Collecting Google Reviews is essential for building trust and credibility, as they serve as social proof of customer satisfaction. These reviews also enhance your search engine rankings, particularly in local SEO, giving you a competitive edge. They offer valuable patient feedback, allowing for improved engagement. A high number of positive reviews can influence treatment uptake, leading to higher conversion rates and organic referrals.

Google review templates

Email one: Send to happy patients immediately after treatment ✕

Subject: **Your dental appointment - 30 seconds**

Dear **[Patient name],**

We work extremely hard to deliver the highest level of dental care to you. As a small and caring team, your Google review would mean the world to each and every one of us!

I only need 30 seconds of your time! Please click this link to leave a review
[Insert your link here]

If you need guidance on your feedback:
a) What were your first impressions of the practice?
b) Were the team caring and did they explain treatment well?
c) How does this experience compare to past dental experiences?
d) Would you recommend us?

Thank you so much in advance for your review!

If you believe there's room for improvement before leaving a review, kindly share your candid feedback. We're passionate about enhancing every patient's experience and truly appreciate insights on areas we can refine.

Email two: Send after one week

Subject: **Your dental appointment - 30 seconds**

Dear **[Patient name]**

Sorry to email again, I just wanted to make sure you received the email below.

We need only 30 seconds of your time. Every review we receive brings us closer to our goal of **[insert number here]** of Google reviews.

We would all really appreciate you helping us to reach our target.

Email three: Send after two weeks

Subject: **Reviewing your experience at [Insert practice name]**

Dear **[Patient Name],**

I hope this email finds you well. Following up from your treatment on [insert date] I wanted to check if you had any feedback for us?

Having not heard from you, we thought perhaps we have some reflecting to do on our service delivery. I would welcome an email back with any thoughts on how you believe we may improve.

We work extremely hard to ensure we deliver the highest level of dental care to you.

Alternatively, if you felt you were given a 5-star experience, then a Google review would mean the world to each and every one of us here at **[insert practice name]**.

I only need 30 seconds of your time. Please click this link to leave a review
[Insert your link here]

Thank you so much in advance!

Build an army of raving fans

Every year, businesses invest considerable time and money to attract new customers. However, many fail to see that their most powerful marketing strategy is completely free. Customer service! You have already seen this with your own eyes with most practices reporting that word of mouth is the biggest source of new patients. If we know that, we should double down on the raving fans strategy.

Raving fans are the patients who go beyond merely liking your brand and become the vocal supporters and advocates of your practice. They are the ones who will not only return to your practice but also share their positive experiences with others, bringing new patients to your door.

In the age of social media, raving fans have more power than ever before. They can share their experiences with your practice on social media platforms, review websites and other online forums, and influence the opinions of their friends, family, and followers.

To create raving fans, you need to provide excellent customer service, personalise your patient's experience, and deliver consistent quality care. Going above and beyond the call of duty to exceed their expectations and make them feel valued is a sure-fire way to turn regular patients into raving fans.

It's also important to listen to your patients and show genuine interest in their concerns and needs. By engaging with your patients and building strong relationships, you create an emotional connection that makes it more likely they will become raving fans.

Remember, raving fans are not only beneficial to your practice's bottom line, but they are also the driving force behind creating a positive and reputable image for your practice. Treat every patient like a VIP, and you'll be well on your way to creating a team of raving fans who will help grow your practice.

ROSE
&
CROWN

Types of patients

Most business either deliver what you expect, or less than what you expect. Indifference is a business killer!

Type of Patient	Description	Attitude	Action
Raving Fans	Patients who are extremely satisfied with your practice and will enthusiastically recommend you to others.	Positive	Actively promote and refer new patients to your practice.
Loyal Patients	Patients who consistently choose your practice for their dental needs and are generally satisfied with the service provided.	Positive	Continue to choose your practice and may refer others if asked.
Indifferent Patients	Patients who are neutral about your practice and may be willing to switch to another practice for convenience or cost.	Neutral	May choose to continue coming to your practice or switch to another based on convenience or cost.
Dissatisfied Patients	Patients who have had a negative experience with your practice and may be inclined to leave negative reviews or not return.	Negative	May leave negative reviews or choose to not return to your practice. May be negative about your practice in private settings.
Lost Patients	Patients who have previously visited your practice but have not returned for a significant amount of time.	Neutral to Negative	May choose to return to your practice if encouraged or reminded, or may never return if they have found another practice.

RESPECTING COMPLAINTS

Respecting complaints

Richard Branson once famously said, 'A complaint is a chance to turn a customer into a lifelong friend.' Adopting this mindset is key to providing exceptional customer service and turning negative situations into positive ones.

Regardless of the size or validity of a complaint, it should be respected and addressed with the same level of care and attention. Taking the time to listen and understand a patient's concerns not only helps to resolve the issue at hand, but also provides an opportunity to identify any potential problems before they escalate.

As a business owner with over twenty years of experience, my first thought when receiving a complaint is always focused on resolving the issue and implementing changes to prevent similar issues from occurring in the future. It's crucial to acknowledge complaints arising from uncommon scenarios and not dismiss them, as addressing them with a proactive approach can prevent them from becoming isolated incidents.

Addressing complaints with respect and attention shows patients that you value their feedback and care about their experience. In the following pages, you'll learn more about understanding and managing patient complaints in a way that aligns with the hospitality industry's approach.

Avoid making negative comments about a patient internally to your team, as it can have a lasting effect on the workplace culture and hinder accountability when mistakes need to be addressed.

Patient nature

A study conducted by the customer service software company Zendesk found that 45% of respondents said they would share a negative customer service experience on social media, and 52% said they would tell friends and family about it.

There are certain individuals in this world for whom complaining is an art form, carefully crafted with years of practice. We all have seen a Karen in action!

Many of us however, either don't complain this often, or when we do, we don't complain in the right direction. Often, we simply complain in our heads or to those closest to us. How many of you have, at one point in your life, received a haircut you weren't 100% happy with but still smiled and said thank you to your hairdresser before going home to cry!?

We're all also a lot happier complaining to our friends or on social media than we are complaining to the person or company that caused our ire. These are called 'silent complaints'. **See page 262 on Silent complaints**.

Understanding that it's not in everyone's nature to complain when they are unhappy with a treatment means that, as a practice owner, you need to be more aware of any subtle signs a patient might show that indicate dissatisfaction and nip those problems in the bud before they've had a chance to sprout! You don't want patients who are indifferent or, worse, unhappy and silently complaining but still leaving you with the assumption that they are satisfied.

Silent complaints

Have you ever received bad service or a faulty product but decided to avoid complaining? I'm guilty of this, mostly with online shopping. Occasionally a product will arrive that isn't as advertised, but when I weigh up the cost of the product versus the time needed to contact the company to complain and/or have to repackage it to send back for a replacement, I simply don't bother. Similarly, I've been to restaurants where the food or service hasn't met standards, but I haven't wanted to burn any mental energy by making a complaint, and I'd instead not go back there again.

I was once asked, 'How was your experience today?' at a top restaurant. I thought, 'Well, since she's asking...' So, I told her succinctly why my experience was bad. I don't think she was expecting it, as her standard operating procedure must have only required her to ask. She heard my feedback but responded with a simple 'OK' and a face that seemed to say, 'I don't know what to do.' While I wasn't planning on complaining, this definitely made the situation worse!

Many businesses assume that no complaints mean good news, but the reality is that most dissatisfied customers won't complain directly to the company. Instead, they may tell friends and family about their negative experience. In fact, research shows that only one in 26 unhappy customers will actually file a complaint with the company, while the other 25, known as 'silent complainers,' will tell an average of 15 people each about their bad experience.

So, it's important to understand that even if you're not receiving direct complaints, there may still be dissatisfaction among your patients. That's why it's crucial to actively seek out feedback and address any issues promptly, rather than assuming everything is fine. By doing so, you can prevent negative word-of-mouth or harmful social media posts and instead build a positive reputation for your practice. Conduct satisfaction surveys to identify potential blind spots. **See page 289 on Blind spots and page 204 on Mystery shoppers.**

WE HEAR YOU.

Be genuine in wanting to help

When addressing a patient's concern or complaint, you must be genuine in wanting to help. Actively listen and give the issue your full attention. Assisting customers when they have a problem is part of our jobs, but showing genuine care elevates you from someone simply doing what you are paid to do, to a caring and helpful individual that your patient will be grateful for.

The way you help someone can communicate a lot. Wearing a forced smile is quickly noticed by us intelligent creatures! We've all had experiences in retail stores where it's evident that the person assisting us is disinterested and possibly judgmental. Being genuinely caring and helpful is essential for building strong patient relationships based on trust and respect.

In the hospitality industry, the use of language is carefully considered. Hotel staff are trained to answer the phone with the phrase 'How may I assist you?' rather than 'How may I help you?' because the latter implies that there is a problem or issue that needs to be addressed. It's a small detail, but it highlights the emphasis that leading hotels place on creating a positive and proactive customer experience—something you should consider.

Lego and the discontinued set

An 11-year-old boy autistic boy, James Groccia, was left bitterly disappointed after saving up his money for two years to buy a Lego Emerald Night Train set, only to discover that it had been discontinued. He wrote a letter telling Lego of his regret and how much he'd wanted the train set. In return, Lego sent a nice yet generic corporate letter of apology. Standard customer service; they at least took the time to reply. However, Lego then went above and beyond by sending a package containing a personalised letter and the discontinued train set for his birthday!

James's parents caught the heart-warming moment of him opening his present on camera. The video went viral, reinforcing Lego's reputation as a company with one of the best customer service values. A quick Google search will reveal many instances of Lego going above and beyond for its customers. According to their group director of customer engagement, Lego operates under their own 'Freaky' ethos, also known as FRKE, which stands for Fun, Reliable, Knowledgeable and Engaging.

By consistently implementing its Freaky brand ethos, Lego can deliver 5-star customer service to every single customer. Now, if they could just make them less painful to tread on..!

LEGO

Remain calm

Remaining calm is crucial when dealing with someone who is shouting or being aggressive. It can be easy to react negatively, but this will only make the situation worse. To de-escalate the situation and address the problem, it's important to get the person to calm down first without saying 'calm down'!

One effective way to calm someone down is to remain calm yourself. Take deep breaths, relax your shoulders, let the person finish and speak slowly and gently in return. This shows that you are listening and that you are in control of the situation. It's also helpful to let the complainant vent their frustrations, as this can help them feel heard and understood. If possible, try to move to a quieter area to reduce any outside distractions.

By staying calm and professional, you demonstrate that you are taking the complaint seriously and are committed to finding a solution. This helps build trust and strengthens positive patient relationships.

Empathy

The foundation of exceptional customer service lies in displaying empathy when handling customer complaints. It's natural to become defensive when faced with an complaint, but putting oneself in the patient's shoes and viewing the situation from their perspective can be extremely beneficial in resolving conflicts. It's important to acknowledge their viewpoint, even if you wouldn't react in the same way.

Taking the time to approach a problem from the patient's perspective can provide a better understanding of their situation and offer insight into how to address the issue. Patients should feel heard, respected, and understood, so it's crucial to listen to their concerns and allow them to express themselves. Practicing active listening and acknowledging their concerns is a key aspect of displaying empathy and understanding, leading to effective communication and exceptional customer service.

While some people are naturally more empathetic than others, research indicates that empathy is a skill that can be learned and developed over time. By treating it as any other skill, one can improve their ability to show empathy, and eventually, it becomes second nature.

Tips to be empathetic

- Ask questions
- Listen
- Be present
- Acknowledge their feelings
- Put yourself in their shoes
- Show care and concern
- Be genuine
- Make eye-contact
- Be accepting of their opinions
- Ask how you can help
- Be encouraging
- Show support
- Don't offer unsolicited advice
- Don't be judgemental
- Don't say 'No one has ever said this before!'

Waiting is hated

Nobody likes waiting. The longer we are kept waiting, the more our customer satisfaction levels go down. People also tend to overestimate how long they've been waiting. A study shows that we overestimate our wait times by as much as 36%! Have you ever noticed that time goes by quickly when we're busy or having fun, but time seems to stop when we're bored or impatient?

Keeping people waiting can sometimes be out of our control, but how we deal with patients during this time can make all the difference. If an appointment is running over and the next patient is sitting in the waiting area, think about how you can occupy their time to make it more interesting for them. Keep them engaged with small talk (**See page 216 on Professional small talk**) and provide them reassurance and an explanation. Show empathy by saying 'I understand you must have a busy day; I assure you it's important to me that you get seen right away'. If they're kept informed, and occupied, they'll have less time to keep checking their watch!

If someone sends an email enquiry you don't immediately have the answer to, make sure to reply. Acknowledge the question and let them know you'll respond as soon as possible. This way, while they may still have to wait a little while for their answer, they don't have to wait to be acknowledged.

Make promises you can keep

A broken promise can make us feel betrayed and disappointed. In our professional lives, it can leave us feeling undervalued or ignored. If you make promises to your patients, you must be able to fulfil them. A broken promise affects your credibility and reputation, not to mention breaking trust between you and your patient.

I remember when my colleague at Digimax once told a client that they would work on something over the weekend. My colleague is a people pleaser, and the client didn't actually ask for this additional work nor was my colleague instructed by management to work on the weekend. Unfortunately, come Monday, it turned out that my colleague's family commitments prevented them from keeping the well-intentioned promise. As a result, the client rightfully reminded my colleague that they had promised to deliver the work by Monday.

When you under promise and over-deliver, you set reasonable expectations so that your patients will feel delighted and valued when you deliver more than anticipated. Promises that are not kept will have a greater negative impact than making no promise at all.

Own your mistakes

We're only human and we make mistakes. But how we deal with our mistakes is the difference between keeping patients happy and losing their trust.

Holding yourself accountable demonstrates that you're responsible when something goes wrong and shows honesty, integrity, and a willingness to fix any issue.

Whether it's dealing with a patient, or working with colleagues, being able to admit when you're wrong, or have made a mistake, can garner respect. On a practical level, the sooner you admit fault, the quicker you can rectify it. Getting defensive or blaming others will only prolong a potentially damaging situation.

I find it preferable when team members are honest about being late, like saying 'Sorry, I overslept,' rather than making up a far-fetched story. Taking responsibility and moving on quickly is key to resolving the issue.

Even if something goes wrong that is out of your control, such as a late delivery from the lab, you are still responsible for delivering to your patient on time. In such situations, it is important to apologise, even if you explain that your supplier is responsible for the delay. Avoid making excuses and focus on finding a way to make it up to your patient. If you believe that making up for the mistake can go a long way, take the opportunity to turn the situation around. While not everyone will need to be compensated, it is essential to show that you are committed to providing exceptional service and taking responsibility for any issues that may arise.

Burberry fail

Even the most successful companies sometimes get customer service very wrong. I had ordered two identical wallets with the same engraved initials from Burberry as gifts for two friends. Coincidentally, the initials of both friends were the same. The brand was impressive as usual, and someone from Burberry even emailed me to confirm that the repeat item wasn't an error. I appreciated the attention to detail and confirmed that it was intentional.

The items were shipped separately, and while one arrived, the other was left outside my home without my permission. This could have been the courier's fault, but since I had chosen the most respected courier in the industry, I couldn't be sure. Unfortunately, the second wallet never arrived. I kept checking the tracking information, which kept saying it would be delivered that day, but it never did. I even missed the chance to hand-deliver it to my friend, who was only in the country for a short time.

I contacted Burberry, and they informed me that an investigation had been raised with UPS and their internal teams to locate the missing order. However, it could take 7-10 working days to resolve the issue. They assured me that they understood the circumstances and would do everything possible to resolve it for me.

When I followed up, expressing my frustration and saying that I couldn't wait that long, I received a 'take it or leave it' response. The team was following their procedure for raising an investigation, and the timeframe was an estimate provided by UPS. If they heard any further updates, they would inform me at the earliest convenience.

Unfortunately, 11 days later, there was still no follow-up, and the gift was still missing. I felt that the company could have acted better in this situation, and the many positive experiences I had with Burberry were overshadowed by this extreme trust withdrawal. Waiting a few days would have been understandable but waiting over 10 days without even the option to request a refund made me feel like the brand didn't genuinely care about my experience as much as I thought.

A luxury brand should know their clientele better and review their approach in a busy space as it could cost them a lifetime of business.

Recurring issues

Pay close attention to what patients say, even if it appears unimportant. Every comment could be an opportunity to enhance the service we provide.

My team has a rule: if we hear about a minor issue more than once, we make a plan to address it – no matter how small it may seem. Often, taking action after the first mention is enough.

Dealing with these problems promptly will prevent friction in our service. Devoting time and effort to finding a solution right away is a wise investment. The cumulative effect of small improvements will yield significant dividends in the long run.

Perhaps your patients sometimes end up going to the wrong practice that has a similar name, or maybe you have seen a patient put their coat back on while seated because the temperature is too low in the waiting area. These are examples of the kind of issues that don't always seem like much but will improve your patients' experience if addressed.

Finding the gift in complaints

In the hospitality industry, teams are trained to see complaints as opportunities for improvement. Although complaints can be frustrating, they can also help us identify problems and enhance the patient experience.

By adopting a positive mindset, negative situations can often be turned into positive outcomes. Complaints, despite their negative nature, can serve as a chance to address broader problems and implement procedures to prevent further complaints in the future.

A complaint from a patient can bring attention to a problem that providers were previously unaware of, whether it be a problem with a particular treatment, a member of staff, or an issue with communication. By acknowledging the problem and taking steps to resolve it, providers can demonstrate their commitment to patient-centred care.

Research has shown that customers who receive quick and efficient resolution to their complaints are more likely to become loyal customers and advocates for the brand. As Winston Churchill once said, 'A pessimist sees a difficulty in every opportunity; an optimist sees the opportunity in every difficulty.'

So, the next time a patient voices a complaint, try to see it as an opportunity to improve. Ask yourself how you can prevent receiving similar complaints in the future. By taking ownership of complaints, addressing concerns, and making improvements, you can create a culture of continuous improvement and ultimately enhance the patient experience.

Fewer complaints can significantly improve team morale and help build your brand.

Identify your blind spots

Acknowledging and identifying your blind spots is crucial to your personal and professional growth. It takes humility and courage to admit that you have weaknesses that need to be addressed. Just like the world's top athletes who continue to work hard to improve their performance, you too must have the determination and willingness to uncover your blind spots and work on them.

Unfortunately, some business owners and leaders are unaware of their blind spots and fail to recognise their significance. They miss out on the opportunity to identify and address issues that may be holding them back from reaching their full potential. Don't fall into this trap – be proactive in your pursuit of growth and success. Be vigilant and keep a lookout for potential blind spots, even if it means taking an uncomfortable look at yourself and your organisation. Remember, the greatest achievers are the ones who continuously seek to improve themselves, and finding and fixing your blind spots is an important part of that journey.

Rather than waiting for your patients to point out an issue you didn't even know you had, be proactive and look for any touchpoints along your patient's journey that could potentially be a blind spot.

Here are 5 steps to help you find blind spots in your business:

1. **Review your operations**: Start by reviewing your business operations to identify areas that might be problematic. Look at your workflow processes, patient interactions, and employee performance to identify any areas that could be improved.
2. **Get feedback**: Ask your team and patients for feedback on how to improve operations. Encourage open and honest communication and assure them that their opinions will be taken seriously. You can also consider hiring external consultants to provide an objective perspective.
3. **Analyse your data**: Analyse your data to identify patterns or trends that might indicate issues. Look for any discrepancies or gaps in your data that might be causing problems. Consider using data visualisation tools to help you identify these blind spots.
4. **Monitor your competition**: Keep an eye on your competition to identify areas where they may be outperforming you. Analyse their marketing strategies, customer service, fees, and treatment offerings to see where you can improve.
5. **Continuously improve**: Blind spots can be difficult to identify, so it's important to continuously improve your business operations. Encourage a culture of continuous improvement, and regularly review your operations to identify and address any areas that might be problematic. This will help you stay ahead of the game and ensure long-term success.

Make giving feedback easy

When someone walks into your practice and says, 'Wow, I love that painting,' you've had unsolicited, positive feedback on your aesthetics. If someone disparages the coffee you've served, this is feedback on your refreshment choices.

Some patients may be too shy, quiet, or introverted to be vocal with their feedback, but their thoughts and opinions are just as important as all your other patients, so make sure it is easy for them to tell you what they think.

Ask patients directly, 'How was your experience? Is there anything we could do to improve for next time?' When you initiate the conversation and open up the avenues for patients to tell you how they feel, they are often happier and more forthcoming with their feedback.

Engaging with patients on social media or emailing feedback forms after a treatment is another way to glean important information on a patient's assessment of their experience. Some people find it easier to be truthful from behind a computer screen rather than face-to-face, so the more channels you offer for them to give feedback, the more chance you have of receiving honest and genuine replies.

At Digimax, we have a feedback form linked at the bottom of our team's emails that says 'Could I have communicated better? Share with Shaz.' It gives our clients direct access to share anything they like with me, and I've found that it's a great way to hear about positive things as well. This helps me recognise team members for their hard work. However, some of my team members like to fill it out with comments like 'Give your handsome programmer a pay rise, he is amazing.'

BE DIFFERENT

ESCAPE THE ORDINARY

Your competition

I've noticed that some principals become fixated on their competitors. While it's important to be aware of the options available to your patients, I urge you to remain focused on being the best. This approach has helped me establish a highly respected dental marketing company that's renowned worldwide. While keeping an eye on market movements, it's equally important to concentrate on your own strengths and improvements, rather than solely relying on what others are doing.

Michael Phelps is one of the most celebrated Olympic athletes of all time, with 28 medals to his name, including 23 gold medals. But even the greatest of all time can make mistakes.

During the 2008 Beijing Olympics, Phelps was competing in the 200-metre butterfly final, his signature event. As he approached the finish line, he was well ahead of his closest competitor and on track to win another gold medal. But then something unexpected happened. Phelps made the mistake of glancing to his left to see where the other swimmers were, causing him to lose his rhythm and momentum.

In the split-second that he took his eyes off the finish line, his opponent, Chad le Clos, took advantage of the opportunity and surged forward to touch the wall ahead of Phelps. Phelps ultimately finished second, missing out on the gold medal by just five-hundredths of a second.

Phelps later admitted that he had made a mistake by looking to his left instead of staying in his lane and focusing on his own race. He realised that in the heat of the moment, he had lost sight of his goals and allowed himself to be distracted by what was happening around him.

This story highlights the importance of staying in your lane, both in sports and in business. When you take your eyes off your own goals and start looking around at what your competitors are doing, it can be easy to lose focus and get off-track.

In business, staying in your lane means focusing on your own company's goals and strategies, rather than getting distracted by what your competitors are doing. It means having a clear understanding of your strengths, weaknesses, and unique value proposition, and using that knowledge to drive your decision-making.

By staying true to your own vision and goals, you can avoid the pitfalls of comparison and remain on the path to success.

THINK
ABOUT
THINGS
DIFFERENTLY

Do what others aren't

What could you be doing that others aren't? The top hotels plan and design these things with careful consideration. For instance, some hotels offer guests a welcome drink along with hot or cold towels, a lucky draw for a chance to win a gift available to repeat guests, special welcome gifts for children, and other such thoughtful gestures.

Here are some ideas to get you thinking about your own list:

1. Selfie smile area
2. Phone charging pods
3. Easy WiFi joining
4. Pre-appointment voice notes
5. Greeting cards for special occasions
6. Educational events for the public
7. Engaging area for children
8. Special gifts for children

Improving the experience is not necessarily about always giving something, but about making it stand out.

Know your USP's

The foundation of your messaging lies in your brand's unique selling propositions (USPs), which should tell your patients why they should choose your dental practice. While some USPs may be obvious, such as quality dental care, there are others that may not be as apparent, such as a multilingual team or virtual consultations. Highlighting these less obvious USPs can make a significant difference in attracting your ideal patients.

Take some time to reflect on what sets your dental practice apart and what makes it better than the competition. By identifying your unique selling propositions, you can create messaging that resonates with your ideal patient and ultimately attracts more of the patients you want to your practice.

Sometimes a practice that wants to be big on aligners is missing key messaging on their website homepage, internally within the practice and even externally on signage. Once you have carved out your USPs, convey them clearly.

Outstanding customer service is about minimising how much your patient needs to have to think about what you can offer them, and why you are the ideal choice. Apple does this very well with their products.

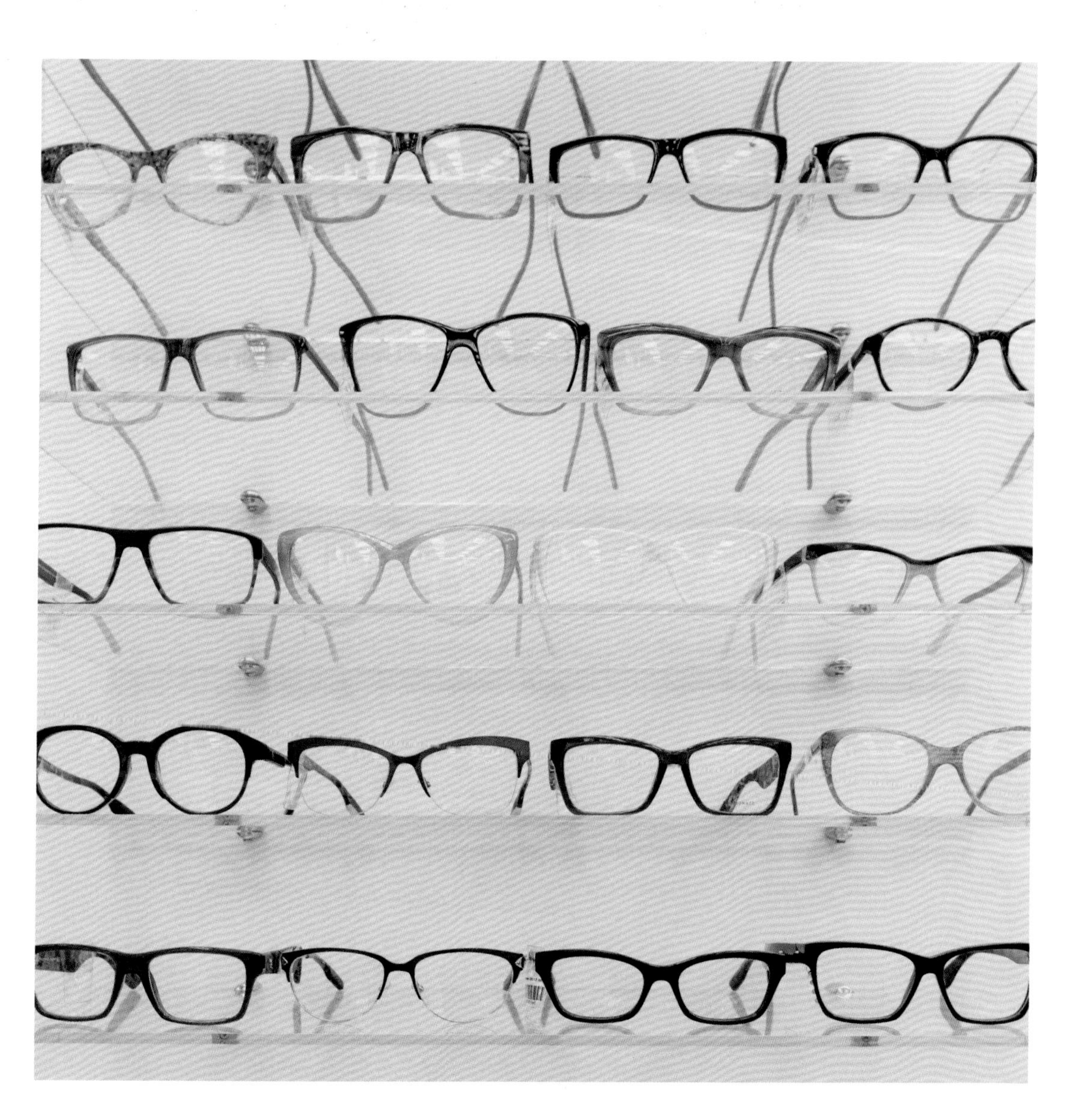

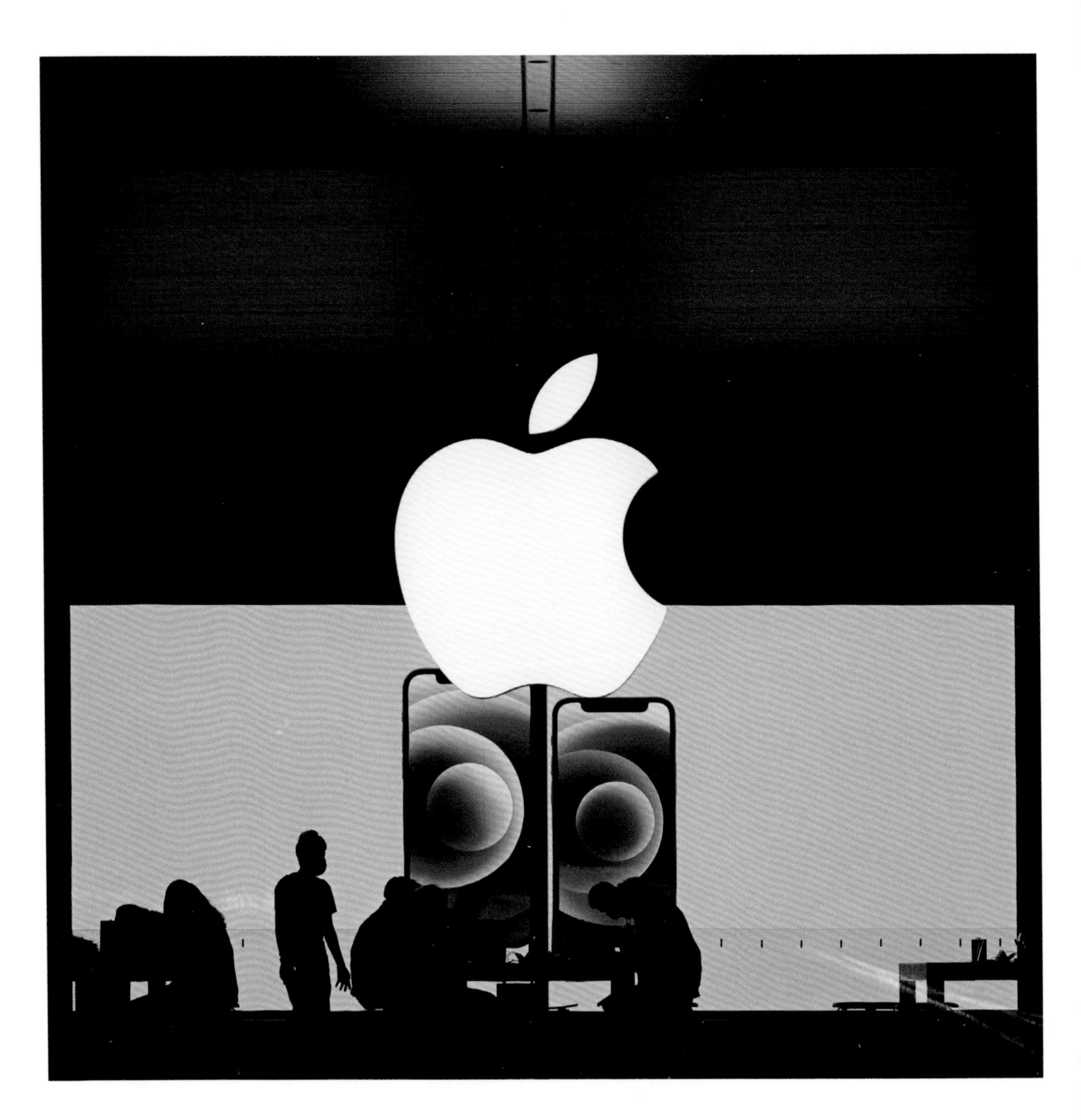

USP Category	Questions to ask
Location and Practice	What makes your location unique? Is there anything unique about your interior that would suit your ideal patient?
Treatments	What treatments do you offer that your ideal patients want to use?
Technology	What technology do you use that is unique or advanced? State the problem they solve instead of listing the features.
Patient Experience	What can patients expect when they visit your practice?
Team Expertise	What makes your team great?
Community Involvement	Do you give back to the community?

Remember, your USPs should be unique to your practice and set you apart. Focus on what makes your practice special and communicate those strengths to your patients.

Let your human side shine through

Making a personal connection with patients can go a long way in building trust and loyalty. Sharing a little bit about yourself outside of the clinical setting is a great way to humanise your practice and make patients feel more comfortable.

Social media is an effective tool for showcasing your personality. You could share your love for rugby, introduce your four-legged friends, or post photos of the interesting meals you cook. By providing glimpses into your life, patients can relate to you on a more personal level, making small talk and getting to know them easier.

More and more principals and associates are embracing this approach, recognising that it helps to build their brand by connecting with their audience. By allowing patients to connect with you as a person, they're more likely to trust your practice and become loyal patients. This applies to all team members!

Uber
Eats

Be ahead of the curve

Back in 2014, Uber launched its food delivery service, Uber Eats, which was ahead of the curve. Recognising a change in consumer dining habits, they created a service to cater to those needs. Today, many food delivery services have emerged, all playing catch-up.

As a dental practice, have you considered opportunities for innovation? What steps can you take to create an exceptional patient experience?

Can you carve out a niche for your practice? Brainstorming with your team and actively asking the question 'How can we stay ahead?' can help you identify opportunities to innovate.

By being creative and innovative with your offerings ahead of your competitors, you can establish yourself as an industry leader, innovator, and trailblazer.

A CHOICE BETWEEN SURVIVAL AND EDUCATION

NO WATER LAND

PRODUCED BY **SHAZ MEMON** DIRECTED BY **SAUMITRA SINGH**

SPECIAL THANKS SANJAY KAPOOR, SHARAD C PRAKASH (KRAZYFOX STUDIO) WRITTEN BY ABHI RAJ SHARMA NARRATION DIVYA DUTTA DOP RAVI RANJAN SHARMA, JATIN WADHWA AND RESHAV SHARMA UK DOP ZACH BUNYAN AND DREW ACTON CREATIVE DIRECTOR OLIVER ACTON
EDITOR SAUMITRA SINGH AND HARDIK SINGH REEN BACKGROUND SCORE JAYANT SANKLA TRAILER EDIT SOM CHAVAN SOUND DESIGN RAMEEZ K ZUBAIR EXECUTIVE PRODUCER HASAN KHAN LINE PRODUCER SHIPRARTZ AND SHUKAR STUDIOS SOUND RECORDIST SANTOSH V SINGH
SHASHANK JHA (SSQUARE STUDIO) AMIT P SHARMA (NAP STUDIO) SUBTITLE ANTARA MEDIA CONSULTANT RITESH SRIVASTAVA (EXPANSION PR/DIGITAL) PUBLICITY DESIGN SHIPRARTZ AND VISHAL KLAIR

shaz.memon

I dedicate this book to my daughter. xxx

#daddysprincess